PROGRAMMING IN micro-PROLOG

ELLIS HORWOOD SERIES IN COMPUTERS AND THEIR APPLICATIONS
Series Editor: Brian Meek, Computer Centre, King's College, University of London

Atherton, R.	Structured Programming with COMAL
Bailey, R.	Functional Programming with HOPE
Barrett, R., Ramsay, A. & Sloman, A.	POP-11: A Practical Language for Artificial Intelligence
Berry, R.E.	Programming Language Translation
Bishop, P.	Fifth Generation Computers: Concepts, Implementations and Uses
Brailsford, D.F. & Walker, A.N.	Introductory ALGOL 68 Programming
Bull, G.M.	The Dartmouth Time Sharing System
Burns, A.	New Information Technology
Burns, A.	The Microchip: Appropriate or Inappropriate Technology
Carberry, J.C.	COBOL
Chivers, I.D.	Standard PASCAL: An Introduction
Chivers, I.D. & Clark, M.W.	Interactive FORTRAN 77: A Hands-on Approach
Clark, M.W.	pc-Portable FORTRAN
Cope, T.	Computing using BASIC: An Interactive Approach
Dahlstrand, I.	Software Portability and Standards
Davie, A.J.T. & Morrison, R.	Recursive Descent Compiling
de Saram, H.	Programming in micro-PROLOG
Deasington, R.J.	A Practical Guide to Computer Communications and Networking, 2nd Edition
Deasington, R.J.	X.25 Explained: Protocols for Packet Switching Networks
Ennals, J.R.	Artificial Intelligence: Applications to Logical Reasoning and Historical Research
Ennals, J.R.	Logic Programmers and Logic Programming
Fernando, C.	Cluster Analysis on Microcomputers
Fossum, E. *et al.*	Computerization of Working Life
Gray, P.M.D.	Logic, Algebra and Databases
Harland, D.M.	Concurrency and Programming Languages
Harland, D.M.	Polymorphic Programming Languages
Hill, I.D. & Meek, B.L.	Programming Language Standardisation
Hogger, C.J. & Hogger, E.I.	PROLOG for Scientists and Engineers
Hutchinson, D.	Fundamentals of Computer Logic
Lester, C.	Advanced Programming in PASCAL
McKenzie, J., Elton, L. & Lewis, R.	Interactive Computer Graphics in Science Teaching
Matthews, J.	FORTH
Meek, B.L., Fairthorne, S. & Moore, L.	Using Computers, 2nd Edition
Meek, B.L., Heath, P. & Rushby, N.	Guide to Good Programming Practice, 2nd Edition
Millington, D.	Systems Analysis and Design for Computer Application
Moore, L.	Foundations of Programming with PASCAL
Moylan, P.	Assembly Language for Engineers
Narayanan, A. & Sharkey, N.E.	An Introduction to LISP
Paterson, A.	Office Systems: Planning, Procurement and Implementation
Pemberton, S. & Daniels, M.C.	PASCAL Implementation
Pesaran, M.H. & Slater, L.J.	Dynamic Regression: Theory and Algorithms
Peter, R.	Recursive Functions in Computer Theory
Phillips, C. & Cornelius, B.	Computational Numerical Methods
Ramsden, E.	Microcomputers in Education 2
Sharp, J.A.	Data Flow Computing
Smith, I.C.H.	Microcomputers in Education
Späth, H.	Cluster Analysis Algorithms
Späth, H.	Cluster Dissection and Analysis
Stratford-Collins, M.J.	ADA: A Programmer's Conversion Course
Teskey, F.N.	Principles of Text Processing
Turner, S.J.	An Introduction to Compiler Design
Whiddett, R.J., *et al.*	UNIX: A Practical Introduction for Users
Whiddett, R.J.	Concurrent Programming: Techniques and Implementations
Young, S.J.	An Introduction to ADA, 2nd (Revised) Edition
Young, S.J.	Real Time Languages

PROGRAMMING IN micro-PROLOG

HUGH de SARAM, B.A., M.A.
Head of General Studies
Marlborough College, Wiltshire

Illustrations by
KEVIN CHAN

ELLIS HORWOOD LIMITED
Publishers · Chichester

Halsted Press: a division of
JOHN WILEY & SONS
New York · Chichester · Brisbane · Toronto

First published in 1985
and Reprinted in 1986 by
ELLIS HORWOOD LIMITED
Market Cross House, Cooper Street, Chichester, West Sussex, PO19 1EB, England

The publisher's colophon is reproduced from James Gillison's drawing of the ancient Market Cross, Chichester.

Distributors:

Australia and New Zealand:
Jacaranda-Wiley Ltd., Jacaranda Press,
JOHN WILEY & SONS INC.
GPO Box 859, Brisbane, Queensland 4001, Australia

Canada:
JOHN WILEY & SONS CANADA LIMITED
22 Worcester Road, Rexdale, Ontario, Canada

Europe and Africa:
JOHN WILEY & SONS LIMITED
Baffins Lane, Chichester, West Sussex, England

North and South America and the rest of the world:
Halsted Press: a division of
JOHN WILEY & SONS
605 Third Avenue, New York, NY 10158, USA

© H. de Saram/Ellis Horwood Limited

British Library Cataloguing in Publication Data
De Saram, Hugh
Programming in micro-PROLOG. —
(Ellis Horwood series in computers and their applications)
1. PROLOG (Computer program language)
I. Title
001.64'24   QA76.73.P7
Library of Congress Card No. 85—5610

ISBN 0-470-20218-1 (Halsted Press)

Typeset by Ellis Horwood Limited
Printed in Great Britain by Unwin Brothers of Woking

COPYRIGHT NOTICE —

All Rights Reserved. No part of this publication may be reproduced, stored in a retrieval system, or transmitted, in any form or by any means, electronic, mechanical, photocopying, recording or otherwise, without the permission of Ellis Horwood Limited, Market Cross House, Cooper Street, Chichester, West Sussex, England.

Contents

Foreword by Richard Ennals	7
Acknowledgements	9
How to use this book	11
A brief introduction	13

Part I — TECHNIQUES

1	Basic Processes	17
2	Some built-in commands	37
3	List Processing	55
4	Modules	83

Part II — APPLICATIONS

5	Games and puzzles	93
6	Augmented turtle graphics	101
7	Databases	113
8	Natural language	127
	Appendix	143
	Index	163

Foreword

This book appears as a PROLOG culture is developing and becoming widespread. PROLOG was first implemented in Marseilles in 1972 for use in natural language processing, by a team led by Alain Colmerauer. Robert Kowalski, then of Edinburgh, developed the theory of logic programming. David Warren of Edinburgh implemented the first version of PROLOG that could compete with conventional languages in terms of performance. It was the adoption of PROLOG by the Japanese in 1981 as the starting point of their Fifth Generation Computer Systems to be based on logic programming and parallel computers that increased public interest in the language. In the previous year, micro-PROLOG began to be available in the United Kingdom on microcomputers.

micro-PROLOG was first developed at Imperial College to enable children to use logic as a computer language. They were enabled to query and develop simple databases, using facts and rules. After the first eighteen months of classroom work, many teachers began to want to go beyond an initial introduction in micro-PROLOG programming, while still using the small microcomputers available in their schools and homes.

Hugh de Saram came on an early course offered at Imperial College. On first using micro-PROLOG he displayed an impressive background in linguistics and some experience of programming in other artificial intelligence languages. He encountered the frustrations of limited computer memory early, and sought to develop the programming facilities for particular chosen educational applications, discarding the 'simple' interface that had been used in early work with children.

Hugh has developed his techniques and applications in the educational environment of Marlborough College. He has drawn on the tradition emanating from Edinburgh in teaching programming in PROLOG on mainframe computers, and this book offers a mixture of traditional artificial intelligence applications and ideas and examples that have arisen in use with students.

Users of educational and home microcomputers will find *Programming in micro-PROLOG* very helpful in exploring powerful programming ideas on a microcomputer. The spread of microcomputers and of micro-PROLOG has meant that the demand for advice from experienced practitioners has outstripped supply. Many books will doubtless appear in the field, but few will match the intellectual depth combined with practical applications shown by Hugh de Saram.

Richard Ennals
Imperial College
December 1984

Acknowledgements

Two people especially enabled me to write this book: Marcus Gray, who introduced me to PROLOG; and Jonathan Briggs, whose direct encouragement to sit down and write gave me the temerity to have a go. In addition, I owe much to Richard Ennals and Derek Brough; to Jon Nichol and Masoud Yazdani; and to Michael Coker.

Michael Coker and Marcus Gray gave me permission to pirate the ideas embodied in some of their Pop-11 programs, but most of the program material was developed and tested amongst the pupils of Marlborough College (among whom James Clarke and Philip Kenyon-Slaney merit mention), and of Preshute C. of E. Primary School and St. Mary's Infants' School, Marlborough. Paul Fiddler and his pupils at Finham Junior School, Coventry, also acted as a remote testbed.

Despite all this help, there are inadequacies of which I am only too well aware, and no doubt others of which I ought to be. For these the responsibility is solely mine.

There is no way I could have written and rewritten the text in longhand, nor would my marriage have survived if I had done the job down at the school computer. I owe quite a debt, therefore to a faithful Sinclair QL, driving a Brother EP44 typewriter. Even with a home word-processor, however, bashing out text is a time-consuming occupation. My wife and family were extremely tolerant, and to them I owe most of all.

Hugh de Saram
Marlborough College October 1984

How to use this book

For reference purposes, this book is divided into two parts – Techniques and Applications. To start with, however, you might like to take it in a different order. Here are some suggestions.

Chapter 1 is really the place to start, since it outlines the fundamental processes of micro-PROLOG. Chapter 2 follows naturally from that, reviewing most of the built-in commands.

From there, however, you could go to the chapter on games and puzzles, and try the insults program. The other two parts of that chapter could also be taken at this stage.

Chapter 3 on list processing probably ought to come next, followed by an attempt to do the family tree exercise touched on at the end of it.

After that, you might look at the chapter on modules and type some of the material from the Appendix into your computer. You would then be in a position to try the chapters on turtle graphics and databases. The chapter on natural language is probably best left till last.

1. Chapter 1
2. Chapter 2
3. Games – Chapter 5
4. List processing – Chapter 3
5. Family tree – Chapter 3

6. Modules – Chapter 4 and Appendix
7. Turtle graphics – Chapter 6
8. Design your own alphabet – Chapter 6
9. Databases – Chapter 7
10. Natural language – Chapter 8

A brief introduction

PROLOG stands for PROgramming in LOGic. Of course, all computer languages employ logic, but the language of logic usually requires translating into some special language that a computer can understand – BASIC, C, PASCAL, or whatever. The idea behind programming in logic is to eliminate the need for such intermediate languages, so that direct entry of logical descriptions is possible. Theoretically, that should make computer programming more accessible to more people.

micro-PROLOG is a significant step towards that goal. It is a powerful, modern computer language – one that is being used to develop the next generation of computers, the so-called 'fifth generation'. Its structure is very simple, yet it can be made to do things that by computer standards are highly intelligent. It is well-suited, for example, to natural language interpretation, to intelligent querying of large quantities of data, and to building expert systems that can learn from experience and act like a consultant in a particular field of knowledge. It is also designed to be easy to learn.

An increasing number of computer types are able to run micro-PROLOG. There are versions supported by the CP/M, the MS-DOS, and the UNIX operating systems. In addition, most computers using the Zilog Z-80 processor can run it. A version for the BBC Acorn computer is imminent at the time of writing, as is one for the Sinclair QL. The examples in this book will be in Spectrum micro-PROLOG.

The language has been developed under the leadership of Professor

Robert Kowalski at Imperial College, London, and is marketed by Logic Programming Associates Ltd. Richard Ennals, also of Imperial College, did a lot of the field-testing in the 'Logic As A Computer Language For Children' project, funded by the Nuffield Foundation and the Science and Engineering Research Council. A notable offshoot of this project has been Jonathan Briggs's MITSI – Man In The Street Interface. Other centres where development of application programs is taking place include Leicester University (Derek Ball), Exeter University (Jon Nichol, Jackie Dean, and Masoud Yazdani), and Marlborough College (the present writer).

Unlike most books on micro-PROLOG so far, this one does not use the Simple beginners' programs supplied with the language. The reader is invited to explore micro-PROLOG from the ground up.

Notes
1. UNIX is a trademark of Bell Laboratories.
2. CP/M is a trademark of Digital Research Corporation.
3. MS-DOS is a trademark of Microsoft.
4. micro-PROLOG is a trademark of Logic Programming Associates.

PART I

TECHNIQUES

1

Basic processes

TEACHING THE COMPUTER: ONE-BY-ONE

Although most computers arrive with various built-in programs, what people generally want to do is to put their own material into the machine. With micro-PROLOG, this is done by typing in a list, which is to say, something enclosed in round brackets. The computer has been programmed to treat single list entries as things it is supposed to remember, and will store them away for future reference. Hence the sub-title of this section – One-by-one – which contrasts with how you ask questions (see next section), where the emphasis is on Two-by-two. Let's look at some examples.

In actual fact, the list that you present to micro-PROLOG when you teach it something must itself contain at least one list:

((This is a micro-PROLOG list-inside-a-list))

Each such list-within-a-list taught to the computer is called a CLAUSE, and constitutes a complete, self-contained 'program', although 'program' is not a very appropriate word where micro-PROLOG is concerned.

When you come to type something into the machine, the latter should be showing the symbols

&.

to indicate that it is ready for your input (the dot means 'I am expecting you to talk to me: please type something'). So throughout the rest of this book, do not type '&.' yourself: it is just put in to indicate what the screen should look like when you go into action. Also, when you see ⟨ENTER⟩, that just means hit the button marked 'ENTER', or perhaps 'RETURN', depending on your machine.

Now let's type in some likely-looking lists, so that we can use them to work on later.

&. ((Queen Elizabeth)) ⟨ENTER⟩
&. ((King Kong)) ⟨ENTER⟩
&.

After pressing the ENTER button each time, the computer should respond with its '&.' sequence, as shown.

Sometimes, either you will hit the ENTER button too soon, or the list that you are typing gets so long that it is clearer to hit the ENTER key deliberately and continue on a new line. When this happens, micro-PROLOG responds with a number and a dot:

&. ((How do you spell ⟨ENTER⟩
2. antidisestablishmentarianism ?) ⟨ENTER⟩
1.) ⟨ENTER⟩
&.

The number indicates the number of right-hand brackets needed to finish off the list, and the dot just means 'keep typing'. You do not have to put in those right-hand brackets straight away: you can go on with the rest of your input; micro-PROLOG is just being helpful in case you have lots of left-hand brackets, and are not sure how many right-hand ones are needed.

Note, however, that once you have hit the ENTER button, you cannot use the cursor or delete keys to go back over anything on the previous line. If you find yourself stuck with an error in this way, the simplest thing to do is to break off your input by using the BREAK or INTERRUPT facility. With Spectrum micro-PROLOG, this requires you to press two keys simultaneously: the 'symbol shift' key and the 'space' key. However you do it on your machine, the result will be signalled as

Error : 11
&.

ASKING QUESTIONS: TWO-BY-TWO

Once your information is stored in the computer, you need to know how to retrieve it, or ask questions about it. micro-PROLOG only responds to two-word 'sentences' when asked to give information: hence the sub-title 'Two-by-two'. If you want to ask something that involves more or less than two words, the designers of the language have provided a way to package them up so that they look like only two words to micro-PROLOG.

Try typing this into your machine (PP is one of the built-in print commands):

&. PP Hello ⟨ENTER⟩

It should reply with 'Hello' on the next line. Now try this:

&. PP Hello world ⟨ENTER⟩

This time, micro-PROLOG will accept the first two words and respond with 'Hello' on the next line; but it will also read the next word, 'world', and take it to be the first part of your next request (it's not a list, so it can't be something you are trying to teach it). The result will look the same, with the '&.' sequence displayed, but in fact the beast is waiting for the second word of your supposed second sentence, 'world . . .'. If you are not aware of this, the next transaction with the computer will produce an error message. Type in

&. PP This is my next request ⟨ENTER⟩

and see what happens. 'Error : 2' should appear on the screen.

Here, therefore, is how you wrap things up to look like a two-word sentence:

&. ? ((PP This is your last chance, computer)) ⟨ENTER⟩

The first word of the sentence is the symbol '?', and you can think of that as indicating to the computer that you are asking it a question. The second word is a list, wrapping up all the details of our request, however complicated it may be. This means that we can put several requests inside this one list, and micro-PROLOG will try to answer them all:

&. ? ((PP Hello world)(PP What's for breakfast?)) ⟨ENTER⟩

'PP' is one of the ready-made commands that the designers

have included in the language, and stands for 'Pretty Print'. Details can be found in the section on 'Human Input and Computer Response' in Chapter 2. Here is another use of it:

&. ? ((King X)(PP X)) ⟨ENTER⟩
Kong
&.

In this case, the computer has gone to look for the list that we typed in at the beginning, ((King Kong)), found out what the second thing in that list is (because we did not know and so put 'X' instead), and then printed out what 'X' stands for. This is a very common sort of requirement. See the section below on 'Variables' for more details. What do you think will happen if you type

&. ? ((Queen X)(PP X)) ⟨ENTER⟩

Try it and see. So long as you taught the computer those two little lists in the first section, you should get a meaningful reply.

SUCCESS, FAILURE, AND BACKTRACKING

The PROLOG family of computer languages is designed to emphasize human logic rather than machine procedure — hence the name 'PROLOG', which stands for 'PROgramming in LOGic'. The thinking behind this is that we are all acquainted with logic, whereas we are not all acquainted with the way computing machines work, so it will be easier for everyone if we can program them in language that tries to reflect our way of thinking.

The particular branch of logic that is used by PROLOG is concerned with testing the truth or falsity of statements (it is called 'predicate logic', but don't let that put you off!). One effect of this is that PROLOG doesn't necessarily give you answers to your questions — it simply tests whether the thing you ask it is true or not, and if you want a substantive answer, you have to ask for it by using some sort of print statement as in the section above with ((King X) (PP X)). This contrasts with some other languages, which reply with substantive answers automatically. Try this sequence of commands (I assume that you still have those two lists about Queen Elizabeth and King Kong in the memory):

&. King X ⟨ENTER⟩
&. Queen X ⟨ENTER⟩
&. Queen Mary ⟨ENTER⟩
?
&.

After the first two requests, micro-PROLOG simply responds with '&.', meaning 'Yes, I know about "King something"', and 'Yes, I know about "Queen something", thank you very much'. After the third request, however, it gives us that question mark, signalling that, although it knows about at least one Queen, it doesn't know about 'Queen Mary'. We say, therefore, that micro-PROLOG has SUCCEEDED in matching the first two requests with lists stored in its memory, but that with the third it has FAILED.

When we make a multiple request to micro-PROLOG, it takes each part in order, as you might expect, and tries to match it with something in its memory before tackling the next part. If it cannot succeed with any particular item, it will not be able to go on to the next; instead, it BACKTRACKS to see if there is another way to match one of the earlier parts, in the hope that this will help it to match the section it is stuck on. Some examples will help to make this clear.

First, let's teach the computer some more facts.

&. ((Prince Charles)) ⟨ENTER⟩
&. ((Prince Andrew)) ⟨ENTER⟩
&. ((Prince Edward)) ⟨ENTER⟩

Now we'll make a multiple request:

&. ? ((Prince X) (PP X) (Queen Mary)) ⟨ENTER⟩

What will hapen? micro-PROLOG will begin by seeing if it can match (Prince X) with any of the lists in its memory. Of course it can, because we have just given it three such lists. Since it checks through its memory sequentially, it will begin by matching (Prince X) with the first *Prince* list we typed in – (Prince Charles) – and at that point, *all* the 'X's in our request are made to stand for 'Charles'. This is called *instantiating a variable* – finding an INSTANCE, or example, which will match the request. It is also called 'giving a value to a variable'.

A

C

B

D

Fig. 1 — Success, failure and backtracking (*continued next page*)

E

G

BASIC PROCESSES 25

F

H

Fig. 1 — Success, failure and backtracking (*continued next page*)

I

K

J

L

Fig. 1 — Success, failure and backtracking (*continued next page*)

Fig. 1 — Success, failure and backtracking

Next, micro-PROLOG deals with (PP X), only now 'X' stands for 'Charles', so instead of printing out a letter X, it prints out 'Charles'. 'PP' succeeds automatically.

micro-PROLOG now encounters (Queen Mary), and tries to match that with a list in its memory, but it cannot, because we have not taught the computer the list (Queen Mary). Therefore backtracking takes place, to find alternative matches to previous clauses if possible, and at this stage the instantiation of 'X' to 'Charles' is cancelled (though not forgotten) in case a different instantiation can be found.

Going back from (Queen Mary), we first meet (PP X). There is no alternative match for this clause: it has been defined as a single-match command by the designers of the language. So we must back up one more stage, to (Prince X).

Now an alternative match *is* possible, because we gave the computer three *Prince* lists to remember. So now 'X' is successfully instantiated to 'Andrew', and micro-PROLOG can go forward again. (PP X) prints out 'X' as 'Andrew'; but then we find (Queen Mary) once more, about whom the computer knows nothing. What do you think will happen? Yes, it will fail as before.

It will come as no surprise to you, I hope, that the backtracking process is now repeated. Yet another prince is found, his name printed out, and yet another failure occurs with (Queen Mary). Now, however, when micro-PROLOG backtracks to the (Prince X) item, it will have run out of princes. There is no other way it can succeed, so it fails, giving us the '?' signal. Your screen should therefore look like this:

&. ? ((Prince X) (PP X) (Queen Mary))
Charles
Andrew
Edward
?
&.

I'm sorry if that is rather a mouthful so early in the book, but if you can form a mental picture of how micro-PROLOG actually works, you will have gone a long way to mastering it. Success, failure, and backtracking are the vital ingredients of a PROLOG process. And although in our example above the backtracking did not enable us to find any way to make the computer match (Queen Mary), in many other situations, it is possible to find a solution to a problem. Try this (EQ means 'equals'):

&. ? ((Prince X) (PP X) (EQ X Andrew)) ⟨ENTER⟩

You will find that the name 'Edward' is not printed out this time. Can you guess why? It is because, at the second attempt to make (EQ X Andrew) succeed, micro-PROLOG is able to do so, and no further backtracking is necessary.

I strongly recommend that you experiment a bit now. Here are some things to try:

&. ? ((Prince X) (PP X) (EQ Charles X))
&. ? ((Prince X) (EQ Andrew X) (PP X))
&. ? ((Prince X) (EQ William X) (PP X))
&. ? ((Prince X) (PP X) (EQ William X))

Notice how the order of the items in your request affects the response of micro-PROLOG, and try to work out why this is so.

VARIABLES

We have already seen some variables in use: the 'X' in (Prince X) is a variable. That simply means we don't yet know what is supposed to be in that slot: 'X' means 'thing as yet unknown'. It may be filled in, or 'given a value', later on, but that value will only affect the clause in which it occurs. In other words, all variables in micro-PROLOG are local variables.

This makes them rather different from variables in most other languages. You do not have to declare them, since you do not have a free choice of naming style. Nor do you have to say what type they are (string, integer, real, etc.). Nor is there an exact equivalent of assignment.

In some computer languages, and in some versions of PROLOG, you are allowed to use meaningful words instead of things like 'X', which makes it easy to keep track of what they are supposed to stand for, but in micro-PROLOG you are only allowed to use X Y Z x y z X1 Y1 Z1 x1 y1 z1 X2 ... etc., up to z127. Thus you could make the following sort of request of the computer:

&. ? ((TIMES 2 2 X) (TIMES 3 3 Y) (SUM X Y Z) (PP Z))

'X' stands for whatever the result of 2 multiplied by 2 is; 'Y' stands for whatever the result of 3 multiplied by 3 is; and 'Z' stands for what you get when you add 'X' and 'Y' together. The values which 'X', 'Y' and 'Z' will take on as the request is processed will only last for the length of that process; they are not squirrelled away in some memory location that can be PEEKed into after the completion of the process.

It is also worth noting that you would achieve exactly the same effect if you followed the request above with this one:

&. ? ((TIMES 2 2 y1) (TIMES 3 3 y2) (SUM y1 y2 y3) (PP y3))

The important thing is that each variable means the same thing throughout any one request, but *only* throughout that one request.

Similarly, variables should be used consistently when giving the computer something new to remember, and it is here that a well-structured language like micro-PROLOG begins to offer advantages. If each piece of program (i.e. each clause) is (a) completely self-contained, which in micro-PROLOG it is, and (b) short, then the task of maintaining consistency is greatly eased. Because of (a), a variable in one clause can have the same name as that in another — they can both be 'X', say — without having to stand for the same thing. In computer jargon, they are strictly local variables. And because of (b), you tend to use fewer of them in each clause, with the result that it is easier to check for consistency. When you think that the major expense in computing these days is the cost of paying programmers, you can see that it is extremely important that languages should be designed to make them easier to program in in the first place, and easier to check through in the second.

So far, then, we have only taught our computer simple facts, but one of the main uses of these machines is to store lots of facts, and then to have ways of selecting those that we want on any particular occasion. To do this selection, we also teach the computer rules — how to select this, how to select that — and it is here that variables are most used, since the rules will be required to extract many different pieces of information on many different occasions, and so will be full of things that do not have fixed values, but can be given different values as and when we need. Let's see how that might look.

We might decide to store in our computer all the facts on a library card index. Once that was done, people might want to extract information about a particular author and the books she wrote, or books on a particular topic. Here is how we might teach it to micro-PROLOG:

&. ((book (Artificial Intelligence and Natural Man)
    (Boden Margaret)
    (computing psychology philosophy language)))
&. ((book (The Bible)
    (Various authors)
    (God Man heaven hell))
&. ((author X) (book Y X Z))
&. ((topics X) (book Y Z X))

In the *author* rule, we are teaching micro-PROLOG that, for some thing 'X' to be an author, it must succeed in finding in its memory a list with *book* as its first item, but containing three other items also, and if it does, then the second item after *book* – the second ARGUMENT, to use the technical term – is what we want.

You can see straight away that the 'X' in the *author* rule does not refer to the same thing as the 'X' in the *topics* rule: in the former, it represents the second argument of *book,* which is the author's name; in the latter, it represents the third argument of *book,* which is the list of topics. 'Z' similarly represents the topics in the *author* rule, but the author in the *topics* rule. As it happens, 'Y' is used for the title in both rules, but we could have used two different variables if we had wanted.

Actually, these rules would never be written in this way, because they don't give enough useful information at one time. It would be better to have rules, for example, that linked authors to titles, and topics to titles. So let's rewrite them:

&. ((author-of X Y) (book X Y Z))
&. ((about X Y) (book Y Z X))

Now, in the first rule, 'X' stands for the first argument of 'book' which was always the title, and 'Y' stands for the second argument of 'book' which was always the author. Similarly, in the second rule,

'X' now stands for the third argument of 'book' (the list of topics), while 'Y' refers to the first argument (the title).

The point is, the *author-of* rule is a complete self-contained clause, and the names of its variables cannot clash with the names of the variables in the *about* rule. Therefore, checking for consistency inside an individual clause is pretty easy, because as a matter of good programming style, we shall try to keep each clause short and clear. Typically, a PROLOG file will contain lots of short clauses, rather than a few long ones.

To round off, try using those two rules. You'll need to have taught them to your computer, and to have taught it also some facts about 'book', as in the examples above.

&. ? ((author-of X Y) (PP X Y))
&. ? ((about X (The Bible)) (PP X))
&. ? ((FORALL ((author-of X Y)) ((PP X Y))))

FORALL enables you to get all the possible answers to a query instead of just the first one (see chapter two for a discussion). Here, micro-PROLOG would keep trying to solve the *author-of* rule until there were no more possible solutions, and for each solution it would print out the values of 'X' and 'Y'.

One thing more remains to be said about micro-PROLOG variables. Whatever you name your variables as you type them in, micro-PROLOG will rename them according to its own internal table of variable names. Thus if the first variable that you type in is called 'y', micro-PROLOG will rename it according to the first variable in its internal table, which happens to be 'X'. It will rename your next variable as 'Y', the next as 'Z', the next as 'x', and so on. So do not be surprised if when you LIST a program that you have typed in, it does not have the same variable names as those you entered. You can make this less confusing by using the built-in symbol that caters for REMARKS – '/*'. For example, you might well type the *author-of* rule like this:

&. ((author-of x y)
    (book x y z)
    (/* (x=title) (y=author) (z=topics))) ⟨ENTER⟩

PREDICATES AND ARGUMENTS

In a micro-PROLOG list, those items that follow the first thing are called 'arguments'. The first thing itself is called the predicate, or relation-name. Thus in the list

 (Queen Elizabeth)

Queen is the predicate or relation-name, and 'Elizabeth' is its single argument.

We have seen how arguments can be designated by variables, either in rules (because they are general-purpose tools) or in requests (because we want the computer to give us some information that we don't currently know). But what about designating predicates by variables? Suppose we wanted to know whether 'Albert' was a *Prince* or a *Queen;* how could we manage that?

It is no good, first of all, just typing

 &. ? ((X Albert) (PP X)) ⟨ENTER⟩

micro-PROLOG cannot cope with requests in that form: 'X' must have been given some value or other before any test can be made. We could do it like this, though, assuming we had the rule for *member* in the computer:

 &. ? ((member X (Queen Prince)) (X Albert) (PP X)) ⟨ENTER⟩

member would instantiate 'X' to 'Queen' to start with, and that means not just the 'X' in the *member* part, but the 'X' in the (X Albert) and (PP X) parts as well. When micro-PROLOG exited from *member,* then, it would be faced no longer with (X Albert), but with (Queen Albert), and would now be able to check through its memory to see if it had a record of such a creature. Not finding one, it would backtrack and see if it could find another solution to *member.* This time, it would instantiate 'X' to *Prince,* and, faced now with (Prince Albert), it would, if we had so programmed it, discover in its memory a record of that form, and go through successfully to print out the value of 'X' as *Prince.*

So there is no problem passing predicates around as variables, so long as when they are actually used, those variables have been instantiated (given a value).

One final word on predicates and arguments: they form a team. By this I mean that

(Prince X)

is not the same creature (at least to micro-PROLOG) as

(Prince X Y)

Note only must the relation-name be the same, but there must also be the same number of arguments if micro-PROLOG is to recognize the two clauses as alternative matches to a problem. So in our earlier examples with the three princes, if we had added a fourth,

&. ((Prince Albert Edward))

he would not have been printed out in answer to the request

&. ? ((FORALL ((Prince X)) ((PP X))))

To get him printed out as well, we would have had to type him in as

&. ((Prince (Albert Edward)))

or

&. ((Prince Albert-Edward))

In both these latter cases, *Prince* has only one argument, even though the first is a list, while the second is a single word or CONSTANT.

SUMMARY

In this chapter we have looked at

- teaching the computer;
- asking the computer questions;
- success, failure, and backtracking;
- variables;
- predicates and arguments.

Together they form the core features of micro-PROLOG. In the next chapter, we shall look at the built-in commands that use these core features.

2

Some built-in commands

This chapter will not be an exhaustive description of all the built-in commands, since some of them are pretty obscure or highly technical. Nevertheless, we shall cover about 90% of them. For the rest, you should consult the *micro-PROLOG Reference Manual* published by Logic Programming Associates Ltd.

HUMAN INPUT AND COMPUTER RESPONSE: R, P, PP

Having looked a little at the theory behind micro-PROLOG, it should provide light relief to tackle the practical business of input and output. The designers of the language, intent as they are on logic, regard the three commands we are about to investigate as necessary evils; that is because they are non-logical. But they happen to make possible what computing is all about – exchanging information – so a brief word will be in order.

'R' is the 'read' command. It causes a program to stop and wait for your input, and it 'reads' that input from the keyboard (there is a more general 'READ' command that can be made to read from any source – see the Reference Manual for details). The single argument of 'R' *must* be a variable.

'P' is a simple print command, and does not put a 'newline' command after what it has printed. This means that the next print command will carry on along the same line.

'PP' does your printing and puts in a newline command as well. Used by itself, it does only a newline command. There are one or two other differences between 'P' and 'PP' which will become apparent if you try the examples below.

&. ? ((P Please input one word:) (R X) (PP) (PP X)) ⟨ENTER⟩
&. ? ((PP Please input one word:) (R X) (PP) (PP X)) ⟨ENTER⟩
&. ? ((PP "Please don't quote me on this")) ⟨ENTER⟩
&. ? ((P "Please don't quote me on this")) ⟨ENTER⟩
&. ? ((PP " ")) ⟨ENTER⟩
&. ? ((P Watch this space " " for more news) (PP)) ⟨ENTER⟩

You will find from these examples that 'P' and 'PP' treat quotation marks quite differently. That will be important when you are planning screen displays.

LIST, KILL, DELCL, ADDCL

One of the things you need to do most often is to list on the screen the material you have put into the computer. To do this, you use LIST plus the relation-name of the material you want – *Queen,* for instance, or *author-of*:

&. LIST Queen ⟨ENTER⟩
&. LIST author-of ⟨ENTER⟩

or just

&. LIST (Queen author-of) ⟨ENTER⟩

or even

&. LIST ALL ⟨ENTER⟩

Sometimes, there is more material to be listed than can fit on the screen in one go. Depending on your machine, there may or may not be automatic scrolling control of the screen. Most likely there will not be, and the first stuff will go shooting off the top of the screen in a most annoying fashion. On some machines, there is a manual control, which you should be ready to use if need be. On the Spectrum, for example, if you keep the Symbol Shift button held down, and tap STOP (marked in red on the 'A' key), alternate taps will stop and start the screen display during LIST.

There comes a time, however, when a programmer gets the urge to kill – program material, that is. micro-PROLOG provides two weapons, one for mass-murder, one for selective assassination. KILL is the indiscriminate bomb, DELCL the sniper's rifle. To destroy the whole world, you just say

&. KILL ALL ⟨ENTER⟩

Alternatively, we could have a local Region Of Terror, and say

&. KILL Prince ⟨ENTER⟩

and all our princes would bite the dust. If, on the other hand, you had it in for just one of the royal gentlemen, you could see which number *Prince* he was in micro-PROLOG's memory by LISTing Prince. You would find, for instance, that Andrew was Prince number two, if you have been following this text exactly; so you could say

&. ?((DELCL Prince 2)) ⟨ENTER⟩

or alternatively

&. DELCL ((Prince Andrew)) ⟨ENTER⟩

but this last method is not often convenient, because not many clauses are quite as short as that, and you would have to type the whole clause out exactly right.

ADDCL is the positive equivalent of DELCL – it adds clauses to the memory for you. You may wonder why such a command is necessary when we started the book by seeing how to add clauses in a different way – by typing in a list. The answer to that is twofold.

First, ADDCL can be used *in a program,* so that you have dynamic control over the memory even during execution of programs. This is of crucial importance, because it enables micro-PROLOG to learn as it goes, and make a note of what it has learned, for future use. See the section 'Error trapping' in part two of Chapter 3 on lists for a good example of this in action. For the moment, we shall content ourselves with a more trivial instance:

&. ? ((PP Tell me the name of another prince:)
      (R X)
      (ADDCL ((Prince X)))) ⟨ENTER⟩

Because of the 'R' command, this request will stop and wait for your input. Suppose you input 'Harry' as the name of another prince: micro-PROLOG would add to its memory the clause ((Prince Harry)). You can check this by typing

&. LIST Prince ⟨ENTER⟩

If you have been following this text exactly from the beginning, the result should be

((Prince Charles))
((Prince Andrew))
((Prince Edward))
((Prince Harry))
&.

The second use of ADDCL is to add clauses to the memory *in a particular order*. Sometimes, the order in which clauses occur is important, and inevitably one types things out in the wrong order just when it is most vital. You can either load the rather large editor that LPA provide with micro-PROLOG, and use its clause-renumbering facility, or you can use DELCL to delete the offending clause, if necessary, followed by ADDCL to insert the right clause in the right order, thus:

&. ? ((ADDCL ((Prince Albert)) 0)) ⟨ENTER⟩

This would add the clause ((Prince Albert)) AFTER the zero'th clause for Prince — i.e. as the first clause for that relation-name.

FILES: LOAD, SAVE, CLOSE

Loading and saving material from and to files is simple, with only one real pitfall to beware of.

To save all the material in the memory, you first dream up a name for the file in which you are going to record it — RUBBISH, perhaps — and then type

&. SAVE RUBBISH ⟨ENTER⟩

If you are using a tape-recorder, you will have to start the thing recording before you press ENTER; with disc and microdrive, you simply make sure you have a disc or cartridge in the device.

You do not have to put the filename in capitals like that, but it is not a bad idea to develop a strict style for you filenames, because when you come to load them back into the machine, none of the clauses in the programs must carry the same name as the file. If, therefore, you stick to lower case in all your programming, and upper case for all your filenames, you will avoid the frustration of not being allowed to load something you urgently need.

LOAD RUBBISH, then, is the equivalent of SAVE RUBBISH if you want to get stuff out of storage into the computer. There is no difficulty over that *unless an error happens while loading.* Sooner or later, however, this is bound to happen, and when it does, you should *immediately close the file*:

&. CLOSE RUBBISH ⟨ENTER⟩

If you do not, you may well try later to load another file, and find yourself with

Error : 6

which means that there is another file open (the one that failed to load properly earlier on). Until that is closed, you will be unable to load or save anything else – and what's more, if you have forgotten the name of the file that did not load properly, you are completely snookered. Well, not quite completely. The only thing left to try is to

&. LIST DICT ⟨ENTER⟩

and see if you can spot the offending filename in the dictionary where micro-PROLOG keeps a record of all the words you use.

EQ, NOT, FAIL, IF, OR

We have already seen EQ at work in Chapter 1. It simply tests to see if its two arguments are identical. If one of them is a variable at the time of the test, then it is given the same value as the other one. The order of the two arguments is not important.

In some languages, this is thought of as two distinct jobs, and given separate symbols. For example, in Pascal, giving a value to a previously valueless variable is called 'assignment', and you must use the symbol ':=', with the valueless variable on the left of ':='; but to test for identicality, you must use '='.

NOT is what you might expect: a negator. You might want to request

&. ? ((Prince X) (NOT EQ X Charles) (PP X)) ⟨ENTER⟩

There is only one slight problem to be aware of with NOT, and that is that it needs some information to negate. If, for example, you had typed

&. ? ((NOT EQ X Charles) (Prince X) (PP X)) ⟨ENTER⟩

you would have gotten nowhere, because the 'EQ X Charles' part would have instantiated 'X' to 'Charles', and then NOT would have made the clause fail, and the '?' sign would have resulted. So be careful of the order in your rule or request when using NOT.

FAIL is useful when you deliberately want a test to fail so that backtracking takes place. Perhaps the most common occasion for this is in defining your own version of micro-PROLOG's error-handler — "?ERROR?" (see Chapter 3 on lists for a fuller treatment).

Normally, when micro-PROLOG is asked to process a clause of which *no* example of the relation-name occurs in the memory, it immediately aborts whatever process it is in the middle of. For a language that is supposed to be intelligent, this might seem rather lame, but in fact you have great freedom to decide how the system should respond to errors: you can define your own "?ERROR?" clauses. An immediate improvement, in most cases, is to arrange for the process to FAIL instead of ABORT, so that backtracking occurs rather than things just coming to an abrupt halt. The following clauses do the trick:

&. (("?ERROR?" 2 X)
    (PP X not defined)
    (FAIL)) ⟨ENTER⟩

&. (("?ERROR?" X Y)
    (NOT EQ X 2)
    (PP Error : X)
    (ABORT)) ⟨ENTER⟩

IF is a powerful addition to the basic armoury. There is no time when you *have* to use it, but it can help to make programs shorter and more elegant. A very clear example of its use can be seen in the listing of the turtle graphics material in the Appendix. The module 'turt-mod' contains a clause called *mv* (short for 'move') which is defined like this:

```
&. ((mv X Y)
      (/* (X=distance)
          (Y=direction)
          (Z=target coordinate))
      (! destination X Y Z)
      (IF (PEN down)
          ((drto Z))
          ((jumpto Z)) ))
```

You can see that IF must be followed by three arguments; note the bracketing carefully. The first argument is a single test; the second one is what to do if the test succeeds; the third is what to do if the test fails. So the IF clause here says, 'IF the pen is down, THEN draw to coordinate Z; ELSE jump to coordinate Z'.

The reason the second and third arguments have double brackets is so that in either case you can specify a string of actions if need be, instead of just one as here.

Sometimes you will want to say 'do nothing' as one of the alternative courses of action. This is indicated by a single empty list. An example might be when you are updating a dictionary of words: if the word is already in the dictionary, nothing needs to be done, but if it is not, then it needs to be added:

```
&. ((update X)
      (IF (dict X)
          ()
          ((ADDCL ((dict X)) )) ))
```

Occasionally, the test you want to do may involve more than one action, but you are not allowed a string of sub-clauses in the same way as you are in the THEN and ELSE parts. You can get round that in two ways, one less elegant than the other.

The first is to use the '?-and-brackets' technique. This enables you to bundle any number of actions together into a single argument for '?'. We have seen it used often for queries that consist of more or less than the standard two-word sentence that micro-PROLOG requires. But it can also be used inside clauses. You will soon find, however, that it is not a terribly elegant way to proceed if you just string yards of sub-clauses together: it becomes very hard to read.

A much better alternative, if your test needs several actions, is to write it as a separate clause altogether, and use its relation-name for the test in your IF clause. You can see an example in the listing of 'gram-mod' in the appendix. The clause 'to-caps' converts any vocabulary you teach your grammar into capital letters, so that it stands out in the screen display. To do this, it has to check to see whether what you type in is already in capitals or not. Here are two ways you could write it; assume 'X' is the letter about to be capitalized if necessary, and 'Y' is the result of that operation:

```
. . .
(IF (? ((NOT LESS X a) (NOT LESS "z" X)))
    ((capital X Y))
    ((EQ X Y)) )
```

or

```
. . .
(IF (between a "z" X)
    ((capital X Y))
    ((EQ X Y)) )
&. ((between X Y Z)
    (NOT LESS Z X)
    (NOT LESS Y Z))
```

I hope you will agree that the second style is simpler to read.

The command OR is useful when either of two conditions is being checked for. There is an example in the listing of 'expert-mod' in the Appendix, as part of the clause *check*:

```
&. ((check X Y)
    (OR ((member X Y)) ((implied-in X Y)) ))
```

Here, if 'X' is either a member of 'Y' or implied in 'Y', then some action will be taken. You may perhaps be able to guess by now that the double bracketing is because each of the two possible conditions may be as complex as you wish — each may contain more than one sub-list, that is. If you make either too complicated, though, it will be very hard for you or other people to read at a later date, so keep it simple, and as with IF, write separate clauses for anything complex.

ISALL, FORALL

These two commands are powerful extensions of micro-PROLOG's capabilities. ISALL allows you to collect all the answers to a given query into a list which you can then use for other purposes. One thing you can do with such a list is measure its length to see how many answers there were to your query.

The section on 'The fox, the chicken and the grain' in Chapter 5, Games and Puzzles, contains a good example of ISALL at work. In this puzzle, a farmer has to get those three animals across a river, but his boat can only take two occupants, one of which is bound to be the farmer himself. The program therefore has to have a way of telling when the boat is full, so as to stop you overloading it. As each item is loaded into the boat, a clause of the form (position-of X boat) is added to the computer's memory. The test for whether the boat is full then could look like this:

&. ((full boat)
 (ISALL X Y (position-of Y boat))
 (length X 2)
 (error boat is full))

The ISALL sub-clause says this: 'X is the list of all the Y's where Y is positioned in the boat'. If that list 'X' is two items long, then the boat is full and an error message is printed on the screen.

In constructing an ISALL clause, you must have as the first argument the list that will result from getting all the answers to your query. As the second argument, you must have an example of the particular item or items (bracketed together in the case of more than one item) from your query that you want put in the answer list. The rest of the ISALL clause can be as long as you like, and constitutes the actual query to which you want all the answers. Here is another example; note the bracketing carefully:

(ISALL X Y (position-of Y boat) (colour-of boat blue))

This says that 'X' will be the list of all the 'Y's that are positioned in boats that are blue (although the colour of the boat has nothing to do with the fox/chicken/grain puzzle).

FORALL is useful when you want a certain action or actions done in all situations that meet a particular specification. You can see an example in the same fox/chicken/grain puzzle, at the point where things are being set up. The puzzle must start with all the objects positioned on or at the left bank of the river, and FORALL accomplishes this very nicely:

&. ((set up)
    (KILL position-of)
    (FORALL ((member X (fox chicken grain man boat)))
        ((ADDCL ((position-of X left))))))

setup does two things. First, it gets rid of any *position-of* clauses left over from previous attempts at the puzzle — (KILL *position-of*). Then in each case where 'X' is a member of the list (fox chicken grain man boat), it adds a clause to the memory indicating that item 'X' is on the left.

FORALL, then, must have two arguments. The first is the specification of the situation in which you want action to be taken, and the second is the list of actions you want done. Each argument can contain as many sub-lists as you like — hence the double brackets in both cases.

STRINGOF, CHAROF, LESS

These two commands operate on strings: that is, not on numbers or variables.

STRINGOF splits a word, which micro-PROLOG normally treats as a single entity, or atom, up into its constituent letters, so that what was one single CONSTANT ends up as a LIST. It also works the other way round, putting together a list of letters to make a word. You can see a use of it in the listing of 'gram-mod' in the Appendix, at the point where *caps* is defined:

&. ((caps X Y)
    (STRINGOF Z X)
    (! to-caps Z x)
    (STRINGOF x Y))

caps takes a word 'X' and turns out another word 'Y' which is simply 'X' in capital letters. To do this, it uses STRINGOF to explode 'X' into a list of individual letters 'Z'; *to-caps* then turns each letter into a capital, and STRINGOF glues the resulting list of capital letters 'x' back into a single word 'Y'.

So the first argument of STRINGOF is always either a variable or a list of individual letters such as (p r o l o g), and the second is always either a variable or a single constant: 'prolog', for instance. Naturally, they musn't both be variables when STRINGOF is actually being processed.

CHAROF is a low-level but still useful command that converts between individual characters and the number code by which the computer stores them — their ASCII code (American Standard Code for Information Interchange). If we dig deeper into the *caps* program described above, and examine a clause called *capital,* we shall see it in use.

&. ((capital X Y)
    (CHAROF X Z)
    (SUM x 32 Z)
    (CHAROF Y x))

This clause says that 'Y' is the capital version of 'X'. The lower case letter 'X' is converted to its ASCII code 'Z'; 32 is then subtracted from 'Z' because the ASCII code is so arranged that each lower case letter is separated by 32 from its upper case partner. So Z − 32 = x. CHAROF then converts 'x' back to the equivalent character 'Y'. So the first argument of CHAROF is always either a variable or a character, and the second is always either a variable or a numerical ASCII code. As with STRINGOF above, when processing actually reaches CHAROF, at least one of its arguments must have been instantiated.

LESS is more commonly used in arithmetic (see below), but it is also useful for testing alphabetical order. In fact, we have already seen it do just that in some of the examples discussed under IF: we needed to see if some letter was between 'a' and 'z'. Here is another simple example:

&. ? ((LESS vamp vampire))

would succeed, but

&. ? ((LESS wet dry))

would fail.

GRAPHICS: NORMAL, HYBRID, BORDER, CLS, LNE, PNT

This will not be a complete description of the graphics commands (see the Reference Manual for how to use LNE and PNT to change colours and modes), but it will give you a good start.

&. HYBRID x

sets the screen to graphics mode, and

&. NORMAL x

returns it to non-graphics mode. Both commands use a throw-away argument.

&. BORDER 2

sets the border colour to colour number 2; you should choose your own colour.

&. CLS 7

clears the screen to colour number 7, in whatever mode you happen to be in at the time. Choose your own colour number.

An example of some of these commands in use can be seen in the 'turt-mod' listings in the appendix, where *cls* (as opposed to CLS) is defined as

&. ((cls 8) (NORMAL x) (CLS 7))
etc.

To draw lines, we use LNE.

&. ? ((LNE 0 0 10 10))

will draw a line from coordinate (0, 0) to coordainte (10, 10) on your screen. It works both in normal and in graphics mode, but in normal mode your lines will scroll upwards with each successive press of the ENTER button.

&. ? ((PNT 0 0))

marks a point at coordinate (0, 0). See the listing of the Blocksworld program in the Appendix for examples.

NUMERICAL WORK

The notation for arithmetic in micro-PROLOG is different from what one is used to, but it is brief and logical. Six predicates are provided.

ADDITION AND SUBTRACTION

The predicate SUM is used for both addition and subtraction.

&. ? ((SUM 2 2 X) (PP X))

will produce the answer '4': the first two arguments add together to produce the third.

Subtraction is done by taking one of the first two arguments away from the third:

&. ? ((SUM X 5 7) (PP X))

Here, the answer '2' is printed out.

So whether you are doing addition or subtraction, the first two arguments add together to make the third. What you cannot do, however, is to have two variables, even if the answer is obvious:

&. ? ((SUM X X 4) (PP X))

Although the only thing that will add to itself to produce '4' is '2', micro-PROLOG does not at present allow this usage.

MULTIPLICATION AND DIVISION

As with addition and subtraction, one predicate handles both multiplication and division:

&. ? ((TIMES 10 10 X) (PP X))

will print out '100' on the screen.

&. ? ((TIMES 50 X 100) (PP X))

will print out '2'.

As with SUM, you are not allowed to have more than one variable when it comes to processing TIMES.

LESS

(LESS X Y), in which neither 'X' nor 'Y' may be variables at the time of processing, tests to see if the first argument is less than the second. So (LESS 2 3) succeeds; (LESS 2 2) fails.

INT

(INT X) tests to see if 'X' is a whole number, or INTEGER (and not a decimal).

(INT X Y) reduces to the nearest integer towards zero whatever number 'X' stands for, and gives that value to 'Y'. Thus (INT -2.6 Y) would give 'Y' the value -2, and (INT 2.6 Y) would give 'Y' the value 2.

SIGN

(SIGN X Y) tests to see if the number 'X' stands for is positive, zero, or negative, and assigns to 'Y' the value 1, 0, or -1 respectively. So (SIGN -3.4 Y) will give 'Y' the value -1. A typical use for this is in determining the absolute (in effect this means positive) value of a number:

    &. ((absolute X Y)
        (SIGN X Z)
        (TIMES Z X Y))

RND

RND generates random numbers for you. You can reset the seed number by using it on its own:

    &. ? ((RND))

You can also set the seed to the number of your choice by using it with one argument:

    &. RND 13

Your most likely use of it, however, is in its two-argument form, to generate random numbers between 0 and the number you choose, e.g.

&. ? ((RND X 10) (PP X))

Note well, however, that although 'X' can always turn out to be 0, it can never be 10 (or whatever other number you give as the limit). The highest it can ever reach is one less than your limit. So here, 9 is the highest number it will reach. You may therefore want to follow your use of RND by adding one to the result.

SOME SAMPLE PROGRAMS

Since I do not propose to write extensively about the use of micro-PROLOG for maths, I am going to end this section on arithmetic with two or three short programs, so that you can see it is perfectly possible to do maths in micro-PROLOG if you have a mind to. In fact, Derek Ball's additions to micro-PROLOG at Leicester University make it a very attractive language for that sort of work.

ROUNDING

First, here is a program for rounding numbers to the nearest integer (rather than to the nearest integer-towards-zero).

&. ((round X Y)
  (SIGN X Z)
  (IF (LESS Z 0)
    ((SUM −0.5 X x))
    ((SUM 0.5 X x)))
  (INT x Y))

POWERS

This program raises a number 'X' to a power 'Y' to give a result 'Z'. For example, if 'X' were 2 and 'Y' were 4, 'Z' would be 16.

&. ((power X 1 X)) /* X to the power 1 = X.
&. ((power X Y Z) /* Otherwise, X to the power Y = Z if
  (SUM x 1 Y) /* Y − 1 = x, and if
  (power X x y) /* X to the power x = y, and if
  (TIMES X y Z)) /* X * y = Z.

FACTORIALS

The program for calculating factorials is quite similar to the one for raising a number to a given power:

```
&. ((factorial X 1)       /* 1 and 0 factorial = 1.
    (LESS −1 X)
    (LESS X 2))
&. ((factorial X Y)       /* Otherwise, X fact. = Y if
    (LESS 1 X)            /* X > 1 and if
    (SUM 1 Z X)           /* X − 1 = Z and if
    (factorial Z x)       /* Z fact. = x and if
    (TIMES X x Y))        /* X * x = Y.
```

TYPE TESTERS: INT, NUM, VAR, LST, CON, SYS

INT we have seen already under 'Numerical Work' above. (INT X) tests to see if 'X' is a whole number.

(NUM X) is a more general predicate, testing whether 'X' is a number; that is, either a whole number or one with a decimal point in it. It is used in the definition of *item* in Chapter 3 on lists.

(VAR X) tests to see whether 'X' is a variable at the time when processing reaches VAR. You can see it used in tandem with NUM in the definition of *item*.

(LST X) checks whether 'X' is a list. *to-list* incorporates it (see the listing for 'dbase-mod' in the Appendix).

(CON X) checks for constants. It is not used in any of the programs in this book, but it could have been used in *to-list* to achieve the same effect as is achieved by using LST and VAR:

```
((to-list X Y)
    (IF (OR ((CON X)) ((NUM X)) ))
        ((EQ (X) Y))
        ((EQ X Y)) ))
```

(SYS X) enables us to find out whether 'X' is a built-in command. It occurs in the listing of 'gram-mod' in the Appendix as part of the clause *body*.

ODDS AND ENDS: SPACE, ABORT, !, /∗, ?, "?ERROR?"

SPACE is useful if you want to find out how much memory is left available to you at any time:

&. ? ((SPACE X) (PP X))

The answer is given in whole kilobytes.

ABORT can be used to cause a process to stop completely and return you to the '&.' signs. It is used in the puzzle of the fox, the chicken and the grain (in Chapter 5 'Games and Puzzles'), to show when you have made a mistake (see the 'review game' clauses). It is also used in the default clause of "?ERROR?" when you define your own error handler (see above under FAIL, and immediately below).

'!' may be inserted before the relation-name of a clause so as to make it immune to backtracking; the clause will not be retried during backtracking. Instead, micro-PROLOG will go straight on back to the preceding clause or sub-clause. This allows you to control how micro-PROLOG processes things, so as to maximize the efficiency of your programs. A discussion may be found in part two of Chapter 3 on lists.

'/∗' is the equivalent of REM in BASIC, enabling you to include remarks in your programs. There are a number of instances of it in the book; the definition of *poly* in Chapter 6 on turtle graphics is one of them.

'?' means 'solve', and takes one argument only — the list of problems that you want solved. It occurs frequently throughout the book, chiefly as an independent command, but also inside clauses; see for instance, the definition of "?ERROR?" in the error-trapping section at the end of Chapter 3.

"?ERROR?" is provided so that you yourself can decide how micro-PROLOG responds to errors, and is extremely useful. One thing you can do is to arrange for failure and backtracking (instead of the normal abortion) in the case of error 2 (see above under FAIL). Another is to cause success instead of abortion for error 13 (drawing off the screen), although this has some slightly funny effects on the Spectrum. Here is how you would do that:

```
    &. (("?ERROR?" 13 X))
    &. (("?ERROR?" X Y)
        (NOT EQ X 13)
        (PP Error : X)
        (ABORT))
```

Probably the most powerful use of it, however, is to enable micro-PROLOG to stop and ask for missing bits of information in mid-process — to learn as it goes along, in other words. See the end of Chapter 3 on lists, under 'Error Trapping', for a full discussion.

SUMMARY

As I mentioned at the beginning of the chapter, this is not an exhaustive account of the system commands of micro-PROLOG. For that, you must consult the reference manual for your version of the language. Even so, those commands covered here constitute the vast majority, and should take you a long way.

3

List processing

Part One - What everybody should know

Since the only structure possessed by micro-PROLOG is the list, learning how to manipulate lists is a central part of mastering the language. In this chapter, we shall attack that goal.

THEORY

A list is formed by enclosing something in round brackets. Here are a few simple examples:

    ()
    (Newton)
    (PP Gravity is a myth: the earth sucks)

In the first example, we have an empty list, and the empty list plays an important part in list processing: it is the invisible last element in every list.

    The second example is a list with one item only. The third is a list with several items, the first of which is the built-in micro-PROLOG command to 'Pretty Print' – 'PP'.

Heads and Tails

Because of the way computers work at the moment, it is always quicker to get at the head of a list than at the tail. List processing is therefore done from the front towards the back. It works rather like a bread-slicer, taking an item off the front end, and very often doing that repeatedly in search of something that you asked for. In micro-PROLOG, the blade of the bread-slicer is the symbol '|': the individual piece or pieces are always on the left of the '|', and what is on the right is always the unsliced loaf left over. Let's look at a specific example.

Suppose there was in the computer's memory the list

(tennis-stars McEnroe Navratilova Connors Lloyd)

We could refer to this list as

(tennis-stars | X)

and 'X' would indicate the sub-list

(McEnroe Navratilova Connors Lloyd)

We could also refer to the list as

(tennis-stars McEnroe | X)

in which case 'X' would be the sub-list

(Navratilova Connors Lloyd)

If we really wanted to show off, we could even do this:

(tennis-stars McEnroe Navratilova Connors Lloyd | X)

and here the 'X' would be our famous empty list ( ).

To summarize the theory, then: to the left of the '|' symbol, you always find one or more individual members of the list; and to the right, you always find a single sub-list containing all the other members of the list. Let's now try that out on the computer.

PRACTICE

Examples

As you no doubt remember, you add something to the computer's memory like this (you don't type in the '&.', of course – micro-PROLOG does that for you).

&. ((seafood clams squid jellyfish)) ⟨ENTER⟩
&. ((poultry chicken turkey rubberduck)) ⟨ENTER⟩

Type those into your computer, and then try this:

&. ? ((seafood | X) (PP X)) ⟨ENTER⟩

The computer should answer with

(clams squid jellyfish)
&.

Let's do that again:

&. ? ((poultry | X) (PP X)) ⟨ENTER⟩

The reply should be

(chicken turkey rubberduck)
&.

Exercises

Here are a couple of challenges to test whether you have got the idea of things so far. Following the model of the examples in 'Heads and Tails' above, and using 'PP' as immediately above, get the computer to reply with

(rubberduck) and   (squid jellyfish)

member

One of the most common things one wants to do with a list is to see if something is a member of it. The program that does this for you is a neat example of several aspects of micro-PROLOG. Here it is:

&. ((member X (Y | Z)) (EQ X Y)) ⟨ENTER⟩
&. ((member X (Y | Z)) (member X Z)) ⟨ENTER⟩

The first clause of this rule says that 'X' is a member of some list (Y | Z) if 'X' is the same as the sliced-off head of that list (i.e. if 'X' equals 'Y'). If, however, this is not the case, micro-PROLOG automatically BACKTRACKS and tries the second clause – backing up and seeing if there is another way to do something is a major feature of micro-PROLOG.

The second clause, then, assumes that 'X' is not equal to 'Y', and goes straight on to test whether 'X' is a member of the tail of the list (i.e. if 'X' is a member of 'Z'). Note that for this test to be done, the whole *member* rule has to be tried again, this time using the truncated bit of list left over after taking off the head 'X'. So we get a kind of circular procession going on, and at each circuit, the bread-slicer takes another slice off the loaf, which gets shorter and shorter. This is called RECURSION, and you will find it used time and again in the course of this book.

Eventually, then, either the first clause succeeds in finding a match between 'X' and 'Y', or the whole list is run through and there is no match. In the first case, micro-PROLOG is freed to go on to the next thing; in the second, it must backtrack or just give up and signal '?'.

I suggest that you type in the two clauses of *member,* and practise using it as follows:

&. ? ((seafood | X) (member squid X) (PP Yes)) ⟨ENTER⟩

and

&. ? ((poultry | X) (member Y X) (PP Y)) ⟨ENTER⟩

and

&. ? ((poultry | X) (NOT member clams X) (PP correct)) ⟨ENTER⟩

and

&. ? ((poultry | X) (FORALL ((member Y X)) ((PP Y)))) ⟨ENTER⟩

and

&. ? ((seafood | X) (member chicken X) (PP Rubbish!)) ⟨ENTER⟩

This last one should cause the computer to respond with '?', because 'chicken' is not a member of the seafood list, and so the *member* test cannot succeed; micro-PROLOG therefore never gets to the (PP Rubbish!) bit.

A final word on *member.* In fact, we can rewrite the rule rather more compactly than we have done, like this:

&. KILL member ⟨ENTER⟩
&. ((member X (X | Y)) ⟨ENTER⟩
&. ((member X (Y | Z)) (member X Z)) ⟨ENTER⟩

FAIL

Another interesting thing to try is the built-in command FAIL. This forces micro-PROLOG to backtrack and look for further ways to solve your problem. One use of it – not a particularly orthodox one, I should say – is when you want all possible answers to some request. FORALL is the more normal thing to use, since it is clearer and more logical (see the section on *which* below). This example is included simply because sometimes it is a useful 'quick and dirty' solution; and it also happens to illustrate rather well the backtracking aspect of list processing.

&. ? ((poultry | X) (member Y X) (PP Y) (FAIL)) ⟨ENTER⟩

You should be rewarded with

    clams
    squid
    jellyfish
    ?
&.

The '?' is because FAIL has caused *member* to backtrack so many times that it has run out of things in the list 'X' to test against, and so the program fails irretrievably – even though it has done all that we asked. That is not logical, and I emphasize that this is only a 'quick and dirty' solution.

which

The more usual way to obtain all answers to a query is to define a command *which*. It doesn't have to be called *which* – it could with reason be called *all* – but the Simple front-end program marketed with micro-PROLOG by Logic Programming Associates Ltd. uses the relation-name *which*, and so other people generally follow suit.

&. ((which (X | Y))
        (FORALL ((? Y)) ((PP X)))) ⟨ENTER⟩

which is defined so that the list which follows the relation-name must have two parts: a head item 'X', and a tail of some sort 'Y'. The 'X' (which may itself be a list containing other items) will be what is printed out. The 'Y' (which may be a whole sequence of lists) is the problem to be solved. Here's how you could use it:

&. which (X (poultry | X)) ⟨ENTER⟩

giving you the answer

(chicken turkey rubberduck)
&.

or

&. which (X (poultry | Y) (member X Y)) ⟨ENTER⟩

giving you the answer

chicken
turkey
rubberduck
&.

You can include any text you fancy with the head item, so long as it is all bracketed together to keep it a single item e.g.

&. which ((X is seafood) (seafood | Y) (member X Y)) ⟨ENTER⟩

giving you the answer

(clams is seafood)
(squid is seafood)
(jellyfish is seafood)
&.

length

It is very useful to be able to measure the length of a list, either to see how many items are in it, or, more likely, as a means to getting at a particular numbered item, say item 2 or item 5. (*length* X Y) is a program that measures the length of list 'X' and gives the answer as some number 'Y'; or alternatively it can check that list 'X' does in fact measure the length of some given number 'Y'. It works very much like *member,* except that it *always* cycles round till it has gone through the whole list, and at each circuit, it keeps count. It is usually defined by writing two rules – a main, top-level one, and a sub-routine that does the real work.

Splitting the process up into two clauses represents a compromise between logic and efficiency. Logically, we want to be able to say simply that the length of some list 'X' is some number 'Y'. It just happens that such a process can be carried out quickly if we give the processor a starting number to work with, but we bury this nasty practicality out of sight in a sub-routine so that people using *length* are not distracted by it.

&. ((length X Y) (len X 0 Y)) ⟨ENTER⟩

&. ((len ( ) X Y) (EQ X Y)) ⟨ENTER⟩
&. ((len (X | Y) Z x)
   (SUM 1 Z y)
   (len Y y x)) ⟨ENTER⟩

The sub-routine called by *length* includes a zero as the third item in its list – or as its 'second argument', if we are going to use the jargon of the computer trade (the first item in a list is usually referred to as the 'relation-name' or 'predicate'). This zero is the initial value of the count-up.

The 'Y' remains an uninstantiated variable until *len* has finished counting up the items in the list. At that point, we allow it to become instantiated to whatever value our original zero has changed to during the counting process.

So when we come to define *len,* it will have two clauses. The first checks to see if we have come to the end of the list we are trying to measure, by seeing if it consists of the empty list. If it does, it instantiates the 'Y' in argument three to the value currently held by the 'X' in argument two: (EQ X Y).

If the list is not empty, micro-PROLOG backtracks to the second clause of *len.* This simply chops off the head ('X') of the list, adds one to the counter, and goes round again with the tail of the list 'Y', and the incremented value of the counter instead of the old value.

As with *member,* we can rewrite *len* more compactly:

&. KILL len ⟨ENTER⟩
&. ((len ( ) X X)) ⟨ENTER⟩
&. ((len (X | Y) Z x)
   (SUM 1 Z y)
   (len Y y x)) ⟨ENTER⟩

reverse
Reversing the order of the elements in a list is a useful thing to

be able to do. Again, we write a main rule and a sub-routine, because we are going to plant a starting seed, as with the zero for the length counter in *len,* only in this case the seed will be an empty list which we shall fill up as we reverse the main list.

&. ((reverse X Y) (rev X ( ) Y)) ⟨ENTER⟩
&. ((rev ( ) X Y) (EQ X Y)) ⟨ENTER⟩
&. ((rev (X | Y) Z x) (rev Y (X | Z) x)) ⟨ENTER⟩

As with *len* and *member,* we can actually rewrite *rev* more compactly I'll give you one guess as to how!

rev works in much the same way as *len,* except that instead of keeping count of the cycles as it slices up the list, it puts each element into another list, and in so doing reverses it. On the first cycle, it slots the first element in front of the empty list that was our seed; on the second cycle, it slots the second element in front of the first element; at the third pass, it slots the third element in front of the second — and so on, until the whole list is reversed, and nothing is left of the original but the good old empty list. At that point, we allow the seed list in argument two to be equated with the variable in argument three that we have been reserving for the final answer.

Splitting and joining lists: *append*
We have looked at the way a list is referred to in micro-PROLOG, and at one or two things that it is useful to be able to do with a whole list — see if something is a member of it; measure its length; and reverse it. Now we shall consider how to take one apart and put it back together again. This is often necessary if we wish to change its contents, either by adding something, or by cutting something out. Luckily, one program does both operations; it is normally called *append.*

First, I'll give you the definition of *append,* and then we'll see what we can do with it.

&. ((append ( ) X X)) ⟨ENTER⟩
&. ((append (X | Y) Z (X | x)) (append Y Z x)) ⟨ENTER⟩

Trying to explain how this works will probably cause more muddle than help, so let's try to learn by example. First, we'll set up a couple of lists to be working with:

&. ((weekdays Tuesday Wednesday Thursday)) ⟨ENTER⟩
&. ((weekend Friday Saturday Sunday Monday)) ⟨ENTER⟩

Now, suppose we wanted to join these two lists to give ourselves one new list that contained all the days of the week. Here's how we could do it:

&. ? ((weekdays | X) (weekend | Y) (append X Y Z) (ADDCL
((week | Z))))

Using ADDCL makes micro-PROLOG add a new clause to its own memory. You can see whether this has happened or not by asking the computer:

&. ? ((week | X) (PP X)) ⟨ENTER⟩

The answer should come back:

(Tuesday Wednesday Thursday Friday Saturday Sunday Monday)

Using *append* **and** *length* **together**: *item*
A particularly apt use of *append* is when you combine it with the use of *length* to isolate a particular numbered item from a list. Here is a program called *item*, then, that gets item number 'X' from list 'Y', and isolates it as thing 'Z'. You could use it to find, say, the third day of the weekend. But first, the program itself:

&. ((item X Y Z)
      (NUM X)
      (SUM −1 X x)
      (append y (Z | z) Y)
      (length y x))

What is happening here? Well, first of all, we have put in a check to make sure that 'X' is a number: (NUM X). This helps to prevent accidental misuse of the program − often an important task for the programmer. Experts call it 'error-trapping'.

Then we subtract one from this number, because we are going to ask *append* to chop 'Y' into two halves so that the thing 'Z' that we want is the first item in the second half; this means that the first half will be (X − 1) items long. SUM works out that calculation and calls the result 'x'. *length* checks that *append* has cut up the list accurately, making the program backtrack and retry *append* until the length test is satisfied.

Suppose, for example, that we asked for item 2 in the list (a b c):

&. ? ((item 2 (a b c) x) (PP x))

(NUM X) checks to see if the first argument of *item* is a number, which of course it is: 2. (SUM −1 X x) gives 'x' the value 1. *append* now goes into action, at first instantiating 'y' to the empty list ( ), 'Z' to 'a', and 'z' to (b c). *length* then checks to see if the first list − ( ) − has length 1, but unfortunately it only has length 0, so *length* fails, and backtracking occurs.

append tries to cut the list (a b c) up in a different fashion now, so that 'y' consists of (a), 'Z' consists of 'b', and 'z' of (c). *length* checks to see if (a) has length 1: it does, and so the instantiation of 'Z' to 'b' is returned as the answer and printed out.

I hope that is intelligible; you might need to read it more than once! Even if you are still unsure about how *item* works, it will be well worth trying it out. So here are some examples:

question:

&. ? ((weekdays | X) (item 2 X Y) (PP Y)) ⟨ENTER⟩

answer:

Wednesday
&.

question:

&. ? ((weekend | X) (item 4 X Y) (PP Y)) ⟨ENTER⟩

answer:

Monday
&.

Sometimes, you may know that something is somewhere in a list, but you want to find out what number item it is. We are going to add a second version of *item*, therefore, that will do that:

&. ((item X Y Z)
  (VAR X)
  (append x (Z | y) Y)

(length x z)
(SUM 1 z X))

This time, we want to make sure that 'X' is NOT a number. Instead, it must be a variable: VAR checks that it is. Then we divide up our list 'Y', again making sure that our thing 'Z' is the first item in the second half. That done, we measure the length of the first half, add one, and we have our answer. Let's try it out:

question:

&. ? ((weekend | X) (item Y X Sunday) (PP Y)) ⟨ENTER⟩

answer:

3
&.

See if you can get the computer to tell you what number day Thursday is in *weekdays*; and what number day Friday is in *weekend*.

Sets

It may surprise you to find the subject of sets cropping up in a chapter on lists, but in fact it is quite in order to think of a set as a list. We have already seen that micro-PROLOG enables us to write a very succinct program to test for membership of a set or list. Here to complement *member* are *intersection* and *union*.

&. ((intersection ( ) X ( )))
&. ((intersection (X | Y) Z (X | x))
     (member X Z)
     (intersection Y Z x))
&. ((intersection (X | Y) Z x)
     (NOT member X Z)
     (intersection Y Z x))
&. ((union ( ) X X))
&. ((union (X | Y) Z x)
     (member X Z)
     (union Y Z x))
&. ((union (X | Y) Z (X | x))
     (NOT member X Z)
     (union Y Z x))

You probably know that the intersection of two sets consists of the list of those items that are members of both sets. In this program, argument three is where the intersection list is collected. So if one set is empty, then the intersecting set is empty as well. Otherwise, if an item in list one is also to be found in list two, then it is slotted in at the front of the answer list, and the program goes round with the tail of the list to test each member of that. If the item is not a member of the second list, the recursion takes place without slotting the item into the answer list.

The program for the union of two sets is very similar. The union of two sets consists of one copy of each item that occurs in either set. Thus the union of an empty set with any other set consists simply of all the members of the non-empty set. Otherwise, if an item in list one is also a member of list two, it is not slotted into the answer list. Conversely, those things only in list one or only in list two are slotted into the answer list. Recursion then proceeds with the tail of list one.

PP and lists
Displaying things to one's liking on the screen is often frustratingly complicated; indeed, often worse than the actual computing of an answer. It will go some way towards easing the problem if we understand the two ways in which we can use 'PP'.

The first we have seen already: using our list for poultry, we did this:

&. ? ((poultry | X) (PP X)) ⟨ENTER⟩

and got the answer

(chicken turkey rubberduck)
&.

But we could also have asked for this:

&. ? ((poultry | X) (PP | X)) ⟨ENTER⟩

in which case the answer would have been printed out as

chicken turkey rubberduck
&.

So it is worth experimenting with 'PP' and the '|' symbol to see if it makes your display more or less clear.

Lists within lists
So far, we have not gone into any complications with our lists, but they can in fact be nested as deeply as you like. It would be possible, for instance, to define *orchestra* as follows:

 ((orchestra
  (((first violins) (second violins) violas cellos basses))
  (trumpets horns trombones tuba)
  (flute oboe clarinet bassoon)
  (timpani (snare drum) cymbals triangle (bass drum)))))

Data are often set up as nested lists like this, and the programmer then makes up little rules so as to extract useful bits of the information according to his/her needs of the moment. We might, for instance, want to be able to pick out one particular section of the orchestra, and ask certain questions about it: 'Is the bassoon a member of the woodwind?'; or 'What instruments belong to the brass family?'. Let's see, then, if we can make up some formulae for getting at the individual sections quickly.

The list that has *orchestra* as its predicate has one argument, which is itself in the form of a list containing other lists. So, using the program *item* that we defined earlier in the chapter, we could make up a rule such as this:

 &. ((strings X) (orchestra Y) (item 1 Y X)) ⟨ENTER⟩

This says that 'To find a string-section 'X', find an orchestra 'Y'; 'X' will then be item one in the list 'Y'.'

 As you can imagine, a rule defining the brass is very similar:

 &. ((brass X) (orchestra Y) (item 2 Y X)) ⟨ENTER⟩

See if you can define the rules for the woodwind and percussion.

Armed with such rules, we can now ask the sort of questions we dreamed up above:

 &. ? ((woodwind X) (member bassoon X) (PP Yes)) ⟨ENTER⟩

and

 &. ? ((brass X) (PP | X)) ⟨ENTER⟩

Note, incidentally, that although we can say (PP | X), because 'X' will be a list, we cannot say (PP | Yes), because 'Yes' is not a list. If we typed (PP | (Yes)), the computer would just note it as (PP Yes).

Updating lists: ADDCL and DELCL

We have seen how *append* can be used to take lists apart; this obviously gives us the opportunity to change their contents. So far, however, I have not made it clear how we can make a permanent change to a list that has been stored in the computer's memory. DELCL and ADDCL are provided for this task: they delete and add clauses.

Suppose, for example, that someone wanted to change the definitions of *weekdays* and *weekend* given above, so that Monday and Friday became weekdays; he could say

&. ? ((DELCL ((weekend | X)))
         (append (Friday | Y) (Monday) X)
         (ADDCL ((weekend | Y)))) ⟨ENTER⟩

&. ? ((DELCL ((weekdays | X)))
         (append (Monday | X) (Friday) Y)
         (ADDCL ((weekdays | Y)))) ⟨ENTER⟩

In the first example, *append* has chopped 'X' into two pieces. The second piece consists of the single-element list (Monday), which is the last day of our weekend, while the first piece includes everything else, but with Friday isolated at the head of the list, thus leaving 'Y' as the new, serious weekend.

The second example uses *append* to add Monday and Friday to the already existing weekdays, producing a new list 'Y' which is then added to the memory of the computer.

See if you can change the definition of *poultry*, perhaps so as to cut out 'rubberduck', or maybe so as to add 'well-hung-pheasant'.

Part Two - More advanced

ERROR TRAPPING

Using CL to find clauses

As it stands when loaded, micro-PROLOG is a bit severe if you ask it to process a clause of which there is no example in the memory (either because you have forgotten to define it, or because you have deleted it): it aborts the whole process. There are two ways to overcome this, of which using CL is one. CL searches the memory for the clause you specify, and if it is not there, simply causes micro-PROLOG to backtrack (not to abort the whole process). Try this:

&. Princess Diana ⟨ENTER⟩

You should get the fascinating response

Error : 2
&.

Error 2 indicates that some clause in your request is not defined — no example of it is present in the computer's memory. In this case, there is no clause starting with 'Princess', and so the whole process is stopped immediately. If this happens in the middle of some large program, it can be very annoying. Let's look at a case in point.

An exercise frequently given to students of micro-PROLOG is the construction of a database about their family trees, and the accompanying rules that define family relationships. Here is a snippet of such a task:

&. ((family Adam Eve (Cain Abel)))

&. ((sibling X Y)
    (family Z x y)
    (member X y)
    (member Y y)
    (NOT EQ X Y))

&. ((brother X Y)
    (sibling X Y)
    (male X))

One of the commonest mistakes associated with this exercise is forgetting to define who is male and who is female — a tedious task anyway if there are a lot of people to document. A good programmer will anticipate and trap this error, and he can do it in one of two ways.

First, he could change (male X) to (CL ((male X))), and add a second clause for *brother* along these lines:

&. KILL brother
&. ((brother X Y) (sibling X Y) (CL ((male X))))
&. ((brother X Y) (PP Not that I know of))

70 TECHNIQUES

A

B

LIST PROCESSING 71

Fig. 2 -- Error 2

In this way, because CL causes backtracking instead of program abortion, micro-PROLOG will find its way to the second *brother* clause if no-one has been defined as male, with the result that a meaningful message is printed out.

An alternative and, in the long run, more fruitful way to handle such mistakes is simply to interfere with how micro-PROLOG handles errors in the first place. That is where "?ERROR?" comes in.

"?ERROR?"

"?ERROR?" is one of the really powerful things about micro-PROLOG; but let's use it simply at first. Type in the following:

&. (("?ERROR?" 2 (X | Y))
　　　(PP)
　　　(PP X not defined)
　　　(FAIL))
&. (("?ERROR?" X Y)
　　　(NOT EQ X 2)
　　　(PP Error : X)
　　　(ABORT))

Fig. 3 — Using CL

What difference will that make? Well, we achieve the same effect as we did by using CL — that is, we no longer get program abortion when error 2 is triggered, but backtracking instead, because of the presence of FAIL in the first "?ERROR?" caluse. But we will get that effect for *any* relation-name that is called by a program without being in the memory, not just for *male* as with our use of CL above.

Learn-as-you-go, or query-the-user
Let us now see if we can build a more sophisticated program that stops and asks us to supply missing clauses during its process, and then carries on with the rest of the process afterwards; in other words, a program that can learn as it goes.

&. KILL "?ERROR?"
&. (("?ERROR?" 2 (X | Y))
    (PP)
    (PP Please define X)
    (PP)
    (R Z)
    (ADDCL Z)
    (? ((X | Y))))
&. (("?ERROR?" X Y)
    (NOT EQ X 2)
    (PP Error : X)
    (ABORT))

In this new version, "?ERROR?" asks us to define the missing clause, adds it to the memory, and then carries on executing the original request — which it is now able to do, since the missing clause is no longer missing.

Do not forget, however, that "?ERROR?" is only called upon when micro-PROLOG is asked to process a clause where *no* example of the relation-name is present in the memory. If there are *some* examples of clauses with the right relation-name, but they just don't happen to be the examples we are after, then "?ERROR?" is not called, and we do not get a chance to supply the missing information — unless we build a rather more discriminating error-trapping capability. Fortunately, that is not hard to do. Let us see how it might be done for *male* and *female* in a family-tree program.

A

C

B

D

Fig. 4a — Asking the user (with answer 'yes')

76 TECHNIQUES

A

C

LIST PROCESSING 77

B

D

Fig. 4b — Asking the user (with answer 'no')

Male and female in a family tree

We shall concentrate on *female* to start with, but it should become obvious that an exactly parallel sequence of clauses can be written to cope with *male*.

First, we want *female* to look for known females on the one hand, but on the other, to stop and ask for information if the individual under investigation is not a known female or a known male.

&. ((female X) (known-female X))
&. ((female X)
        (NOT known-female X)
        (NOT known-male X)
        (IF (find X is a female)
        ((ADDCL (found female X))))
        ((ADDCL (found male X))) (FAIL))))

You will see that if 'X' is not found to be a female, the implication that he is therefore male is not wasted: the individual is added to the memory as male. But the clause must then be made to fail, since this is, after all, a test of whether someone is female!

It remains to define *known-female, known-male,* and *find.* First, *known-female.* To begin with, it is safe to assume that all mothers are female, and we have a ready source of information about who is a mother: the *family* clauses in our database; here, we have chosen to place the mother as the second argument each time. But there may well be a second source of information, too: anyone added to the memory as *found female* by a previous use of the program. So

&. ((known-female X) (family Y X Z))
&. ((known-female X) (CL ((found female X))))

&. ((known-male X) (family X Y Z))
&. ((known-male X) (CL ((found male X))))

Notice that we use CL in the second *found* clause, because on the first use of the program, when no-one will have been 'found female', we do not want to trigger the "?ERROR?" clause; instead, we want micro-PROLOG to keep processing *female* by now backtracking to its second clause.

Now for *find*: if the person under investigation is not known to be female nor known to be male, we want the program to stop and ask the user.

&. ((find X is a female)
  (PP)
  (PP Is X a female?)
  (PP Please type yes or no:)
  (R Y)
  (EQ Y yes))

Notice that if the user answers yes to the question 'Is X a female?', then the *find* program succeeds, causing the *female* clause to add 'X' to the memory as having been 'found female'. If the user's answer is anything other than 'yes', then *find* fails, and the *female* clause has to use the ELSE section of its IF clause, adding 'X' to the memory as having been *found male,* and then failing.

In fact, we can write a more general *find* clause that will work for either *male* or *female*:

&. KILL find
&. ((find X Y | Z)
  (PP)
  (P Y X | Z) (PP ?)
  (PP Please type yes or no)
  (R x)
  (EQ x yes))

Two warnings. First, do not ask people to type y or n instead of yes or no. The reason for this is that micro-PROLOG reads y as a variable, not as an alphabetical letter. A user would therefore have to go to the trouble of typing "y" rather than y. Second, it won't work if you write (R yes), rather than (R x) (EQ x yes).

All that is left to do now is to define a pair of *male* clauses that is exactly the same as the *female* ones, but with the sexes switched around.

In this sequence of programs, then, there are examples of most aspects of error trapping.

(1) There is the use of CL to forestall "?ERROR?" in particular selected cases.
(2) There is the use of the learn-as-you-go idea, in *find.*

80 TECHNIQUES

(3) If we include the latest "?ERROR?" definition above, there is the use of "?ERROR?" as a catch-all safety net for forgotten definitions.

It adds up to quite a comprehensive capability.

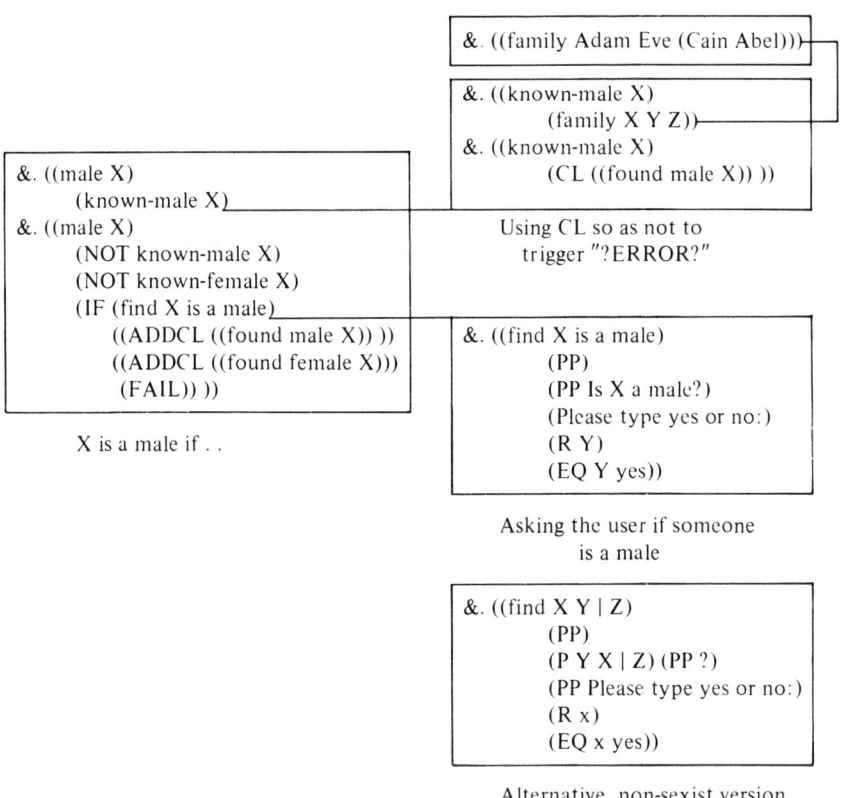

Fig. 5 — Asking the user

EFFICIENCY IN LIST PROCESSING
Controlling backtracking, using '!'
We have seen that backtracking causes micro-PROLOG to retrace its steps, retrying each sub-clause in case a different solution is possible. We have also seen that some of the built-in commands such as PP

have been defined as non-repeating – backtracking just skates over PP without the printing being done again. Occasionally, it is useful to be able to arrange for this to happen with clauses that we ourselves have defined, and '!' is provided for that purpose.

You can see it used inside the clause *check-out* which forms part of the expert system module (listed in the Appendix). *check-out* is defined as follows:

&. ((check-out X Y Z)
      (! check Z)
      (consultation X Y Z))

Suppose 'Z' was a list of symptoms for a disease. *consultation* would go through the list, asking you, the user, if each symptom applies to you. If they all do, then you probably have disease 'Y', whatever that may be. If, however, you do not, the expert will go back to its store of knowledge about diseases, fish out another nasty example, and try that list of symptoms on you. But first, to save asking you the same question twice, it does a check to see whether your answers from the previous consultation (which it has made a careful note of) rule out this new disease.

Now, what we don't want to happen is for this *check* to be repeated during any backtracking that occurs after a failed consultation. That would mean that a list of symptoms could be checked twice – once on the way into a consultation, and once more on the way out during backtracking from an unsuccessful consultation. Such duplication of effort is wasteful.

So we include '!' before *check*, to tell micro-PROLOG to skate over it on backtracking. Now it will only ever be used on the journey into the consultation, and never on the journey back after a failure.

Rule ordering: tail recursion
Before launching into this section, I'd like to highlight two of the features of micro-PROLOG that you will need to keep in mind as we go. The first is the fact that, in order to be able to backtrack when necessary, to try alternative ways of solving a problem, micro-PROLOG piles up a stack of notes in its memory about what solutions it has already tried. So *remember the stack*. Secondly, remember also

that in many processes, we use clauses that re-call themselves — that use recursion, in other words — in order to repeat an action lots of times. So *remember recursion.*

Now think for a minute about what happens to the size of the stack when a large recursion is going on: it gets very large very quickly. If we are not careful, the computer will run out of space before it has done its job. The designers of the language have therefore very kindly given us a way to tell the processor when we don't want it to worry about building a stack: tail recursion.

Tail recursion is when we process a list by chopping off the head, taking the tail, and going round to repeat the same process. *member, length, reverse,* and *append* all use it.

It would be quite possible to write these rules in a different order, e.g.:

((len (X | Y) Z x) (SUM 1 Z y) (len Y y x))
((len ( ) X X))

However, it happens to be much more economical on use of memory if we describe the final condition first, and the more general state second:

((len ( ) X X))
((len (X | Y) Z y) (SUM 1 Z x) (len Y y x))

At each circuit made by *len,* micro-PROLOG tests for the final condition first. That indicates to it that it has no need to keep track of its efforts by piling up a stack of notes, and so the whole process uses no extra space in the memory. This arrangement is particular for tail-recursion of lists. Appendix D of the Spectrum micro-PROLOG Reference Manual gives a thorough, if rather technical, explanation.

SUMMARY

The list, then, has been found by computer language designers to be an immensely fruitful and powerful structure, and learning to handle it with skill and subtlety is worth a lot of effort and patient experimentation. In the second half of the book — Applications — you will see the list used to tackle a wide variety of tasks.

4

Modules

One of the outstandingly useful facilities offered by micro-PROLOG is the module. A module is a collection of program clauses stored in an area of the computer's memory to which there is only restricted access; and the importance of that is as follows.

However much planning one does beforehand, developing programs involves mistakes, changes of mind, and scrapping of material. It is important to be able to do this scrapping quickly and cleanly, while at the same time preserving the clauses that you want to keep.

Alternatively, you may have written some programs that are applicable to more than one set of data. When KILLing the first set of data before LOADing the second, you will want not to KILL the control clauses.

In brief, we want to be able to say

&. KILL ALL ⟨ENTER⟩

without actually KILLing everything. To escape the angel of death, use a module.

CRMOD, CLMOD, OPMOD, EXPORTS AND IMPORTS

CRMOD is used to CReate MODules; CLMOD to close them; and OPMOD to open them. The restricted access mentioned above is implemented by allowing only designated clauses from the module to have effect in the public part of the memory, and only designated words from the public part of the memory to have effect inside the module. These two sets of information are stored in an EXPORT LIST and an IMPORT LIST respectively, and must form the first clause of any module.

When you save a module in a disk or tape file, the first thing to be saved is the clause indicating that the material that follows is a module, not an ordinary program file. This is also the clause which contains the export and import lists. Thus when later you load the file in which the module is stored, the first thing micro-PROLOG reads off the tape or disc is this clause, and the system takes appropriate action: it sets aside an area of memory for the exclusive use of the module clauses, and stores them there.

It is for this reason that the computer shows '&' as well as '.' – the '&' shows that you are working in the public area of the memory. If you use CRMOD or OPMOD, that enables you to work in the restricted area of the memory (perhaps to tinker with a module clause, for example), and the computer will no longer show '&', but the module name.

Here, then, is the world's simplest module – and probably the world's most useful: a tiny editor. Although LPA provide a nice editor along with micro-PROLOG, it is rather large. I prefer to have one that I can keep loaded most of the time, since it takes up next to no space.

&. ? ((CRMOD ed-mod (ed) ( ))) ⟨ENTER⟩

ed-mod. ((ed X)
       (R Y)
       (CL ((X | Z) | x) Y Y)
       (RFILL (((X | Z) | x)) y)
       (ADDCL y Y)
       (DELCL X Y)) ⟨ENTER⟩

ed-mod. CLMOD x ⟨ENTER⟩

&. ? ((SAVE ED ed-mod)) ⟨ENTER⟩

There are a number of things worth noting here. First of all, CRMOD must have three arguments. As argument one, there must be the module name. And it is worth developing a set style for your module names. The standard way is to choose the word that best describes the general purpose of the module, and stick '-mod' on the end of it. Linked to that, moreover, is the name of the disc or tape file that you store it in, which is normally the capital-letter version of the word that you thought up to describe the module; e.g. for 'ed-mod' we have the file ED. Whatever style you choose, make sure that the file name is distinct from the module name, and that both of these are distinct from any of the relation-names present in the computer, either now or later, when the module is loaded.

The second argument of CRMOD must be the export list. In the case of 'ed-mod', that is simple − (ed) − but most modules export more than one relation-name. You must include all the relation-names of the module clauses that you will want to use when working in the public area (which is where you will normally be). If you look at the export and import lists of the modules in the Appendix, you will get a clearer picture.

The third argument must be the import list. In our example, there is nothing to import, but we must still write the empty list: three arguments are required, whether or not the last two contain anything. Included in this list must be all the WORDS − not just all the relation-names − which will be used by the clauses inside the module but which are not in the export list. Numbers, on the other hand, do not need to be imported. Again, look at the examples in the Appendix. It will probably take you a little while to get good at this part of the game.

Notice now how the computer's prompt changes once we have used CRMOD: it gives us the module name, followed by '.', to indicate that we are dealing with an area of the memory set aside for this module, and not the public area signalled by '&'.

With the use of CLMOD, the prompt reverts to '&.' again − we are automatically tipped back into the public area. CLMOD itself must have one argument, but it does not matter what it is. It is just there to make up the famous micro-PROLOG two-word sentence; otherwise we would have had to use the '?'-and-brackets packaging trick. That is a useful ploy for you to remember when you come to do your own programming: the throw-away argument.

By contrast, when we SAVE a module, we do have to do the packaging trick, because SAVE has to have two arguments − the name of the file (ED) and the name of the module ('ed-mod').

If you ever want to get back inside the module, to change something, you will have to use OPMOD; e.g.

&. OPMOD ed-mod ⟨ENTER⟩

To see what is inside a module, you can, for example,

&. LIST ed-mod ⟨ENTER⟩

or you can open the module using OPMOD and LIST ALL. To get rid of a module, you type, for example,

&. KILL ed-mod ⟨ENTER⟩

So much for the generalities of module-building; what about 'ed' itself? There is an interesting trick employed, you see, to enable us when using 'ed' to avoid the great packaging fiasco. The secret is in the 'R' statement. What this does is allow us to enter a third word after our standard two-word sentence; because when we edit a clause, we need (with this editor) to know which example of the clause we are going to edit — the first, the second, or what. The number can be found by LISTing the relation-name, and counting. So, for example, with the 'Prince' relation-name from Chapter 4, we could

&. LIST Prince ⟨ENTER⟩

decide what number Prince we wanted to edit (we'll choose Edward, who I think was Prince number three), and type

&. ed Prince 3 ⟨ENTER⟩

So that, too, is a useful trick if you want to avoid the dreaded '?'-and-brackets. However, it is not a widely applicable trick, since it can only be resorted to with a clause you are never going to include in a multiple request, or as a sub-clause inside another, bigger clause. Fortunately, 'ed' is such a creature: it is only ever going to be used by itself.

LONGER MODULES

It is not often that you can type a module straight in like that. Normally, you will develop and test the material gradually in the public part of the memory, then when you are satisfied that it all works as you want it to, you decide to wrap it up as a module.

To do this, you can SAVE the clauses you want in a temporary file, create the module as before, using CRMOD, and then LOAD the temporary file instead of typing in everything by hand. Again, it is better to have nothing else loaded while you do this, in case of relation-name clashes, although if you are sure there will be none then you can try it with other material on board. If you do get *any* error while saving or loading, *remember to* CLOSE *the file.* Otherwise you will probably find yourself later with

    Error : 6

on the screen, meaning 'File left open'. If you are unfortunate enough to have

    Error : 12

flashed at you, that means you have a name clash between something in your module's import or export list and a clause already on board.

Saving the clauses in a temporary file can be done two ways. Either you can kill off everything else but the clauses you want; or you can use SAVE in its selective format:

    &. ? ((SAVE TEMP (author-of about))) ⟨ENTER⟩

This saves just those named relation-names in the file TEMP.

EDITING A MODULE

At this point it will pay you to turn to the Appendix and study some of the modules listed there. You will notice, for instance, that nearly all of them import 'ed', so that alterations can be made to the module clauses. To edit something inside a module, you first open it; for example:

    &. OPMOD turt-mod ⟨ENTER⟩
    turt-mod. ed jumpto 1 ⟨ENTER⟩
    etc.
    turt-mod. CLMOD x ⟨ENTER⟩
    &.

ALTERING THE EXPORT AND IMPORT LISTS

It is perfectly all right to use an editor to alter existing clauses in a module. You can also add a clause that you do not want to feature in the import or export list (you must, of course, SAVE this new version if you want a permanent record of it). But if you wish to add a new clause that you want the general public to use, and which therefore needs to appear in the export list, or if you have left a word out of the import list, things get more complicated.

You cannot just edit the export or import list. You have to open the module using OPMOD, and SAVE the module clauses in a temporary file. For instance,

&. OPMOD ed-mod ⟨ENTER⟩

ed-mod. SAVE TEMP ⟨ENTER⟩

That done, close the module using CLMOD. Make sure you have a complete list of the export and import lists by LISTing the module and writing them down on a piece of paper if necessary.

ed-mod. CLMOD x ⟨ENTER⟩

&. LIST ed-mod ⟨ENTER⟩

Follow this by interrupting the screen display (because you only want the first clause of the module), and clearing the module from memory. Interrupting will signal on the screen

Error : 11

Now you type

&. KILL ed-mod ⟨ENTER⟩
&. SPACE x ⟨ENTER⟩   /∗ This clears the system DICTionary

Using SPACE to clear out the system dictionary greatly reduces the chance of name clashes when you recreate your module. Once you have used CRMOD, then, to set up your new export and import lists, you can LOAD back the contents of the temporary file, and use CLMOD to close the module. And of course you will have to SAVE this new module as such, overwriting your old version.

&. ? ((CRMOD ed-mod . . . ⟨ENTER⟩

ed-mod. LOAD TEMP ⟨ENTER⟩
ed-mod. CLMOD x ⟨ENTER⟩

&. ? ((SAVE ED ed-mod)) ⟨ENTER⟩

A PRACTICE EXERCISE

You might like now to try designing and using a short module of your own. You could, perhaps, write a sort of utilities module, containing such things as *append, member, length, reverse* and *item.* Be prepared to stick at it till it works: your effort will pay huge dividends in the long run.

PART II
APPLICATIONS

5

Games and puzzles

INSULTS

One of the programs that seems to go down well with the classes I have taught is this insult generator. It is a straight translation of a Pop-11 program originally written by Marcus Gray and Michael Coker, neither of whom is particularly keen to take credit for it.

It uses three collections of insult-parts, from which random choices are made. The parts are then strung together to make a coherent insult-whole, and printed out in endlessly repeating succession. Adding to the assortment of insult-parts in your own particular style is what this exercise is all about. When you want to stop the stream of invective, use the interrupt facility provided on your machine. In the case of the Spectrum, that means pressing the symbol shift key and the space key at the same time.

&. ((insult X) (! insult))

&. ((insult)
   (oneof list1 X)
   (oneof list2 Y)
   (oneof list3 Z)
   (pr-lists(X Y Z))
   (insult))

94 APPLICATIONS

&. ((list1
    (Get lost)
    (Go play on the freeway)
    (Naff off)))

&. ((list2
    (you cretinous)
    (you perverted)
    (you under-developed)))

&. ((list3
    (cod piece)
    (hamburger bun)
    (rotten cabbage)))

&. ((oneof X Y)
    (X | Z)
    (length Z x)
    (RND y x)
    (next-item y Z Y))

&. ((next-item X Y Z)
    (append x (Z | y) Y)
    (length x X))

&. ((length X Y) (len X 0 Y))

&. ((len ( ) X X))
&. ((len (X | Y) Z x) (SUM 1 Z y) (len Y y x))

&. ((append ( ) X X))
&. ((append (X | Y) Z (X | x)) (append Y Z x))

&. ((pr-lists ( )) (PP))
&. ((pr-lists (X | Y))
    (P | X)
    (P " ")
    (pr-lists Y))

To run this program, you simply type
    &. insult x ⟨ENTER⟩

Note that the top-level command (insult x) uses a throw-away argument, to save having to employ the packaging technique. To tailor things to your heart's desire, all you need do is load the editor and modify the three insult lists. Or you could, of course, go further and make more elaborate insults consisting of four or five pieces, adjusting the *insult* part of the program accordingly.

The very simple principle illustrated here — that of stringing together phrases to make a sentence — is taken a good deal further in Chapter 8, on Natural Language.

THE FOX, THE CHICKEN, AND THE GRAIN

The problem of how a farmer gets the three items in the title across a river, one by one, is a classic puzzle in its own right, but it is also ideally adapted to the computer, since it combines the need for logical thinking with some rather repetitive actions. If the farmer leaves the fox with the chicken, the chicken will get eaten; if he leaves the grain with the chicken, that will get eaten, too. But his boat only has room for himself and one other item. How can he get them all across? Here are the clauses that give you the tools to construct a solution.

&. ((start X)
   (/* X is a throw-away argument)
   (setup)
   (view X)

&. ((setup)
   (KILL position-of)
   (FORALL ((member X (man boat for chicken grain)))
       ((ADDCL ((position-of X left))))))

&. ((member X (X | Y)))

&. ((member X (Y | Z)) (member X Z))

&. ((view X)
   (/* X is a throw-away argument)
   (PP)
   (LIST position-of)

&. ((get in)
   (NOT full boat)
   (position-of boat X)
   (reposition man X boat)
   (review game))

&. ((get in)
    (position-of man boat)
    (error man already in boat)

&. ((reposition X Y Z)
    (DELCL ((position-of X Y)))
    (ADDCL ((position-of X Z)))))

&. ((get out)
    (position-of boat X)
    (reposition man boat X)
    (review game))

&. ((get out)
    (NOT position-of man boat)
    (error man not in boat))

&. ((row across)
    (position-of man boat)
    (make trip)
    (review game))

&. ((row across)
    (NOT position-of man boat)
    (error man not in boat))

&. ((make trip)
    (other-bank X Y)
    (reposition boat X Y)))

&. ((other-bank left right))
&. ((other-bank right left))

&. ((error | X)
    (PP) (PP Sorry: | X) (PP) (ABORT))

&. ((full boat)
    (ISALL (X Y) Z (position-of Z boat))
    (error boat is full))

&. ((load man)
    (error man cannot load himself))

&. ((load X)
    (NOT EQ X man)
    (NOT full boat)
    (position-of boat Y)

```
            (position-of man Y)
            (reposition X Y boat)
            (review game))
   &. ((load X)
            (position-of X Y)
            (position-of boat Z)
            (other-bank Y Z)
            (error X across river))
   &. ((load X)
            (position-of X boat)
            (error X already in boat))
   &. ((unload man)
            (error man cannot unload himself))
   &. ((unload X)
            (position-of boat Y)
            (position-of man Y)
            (reposition X boat Y)
            (review game))
   &. ((unload X)
            (NOT position-of X boat)
            (error X is not in boat)
   &. ((unload X)
            (position-of man boat)
            (error man must get out first))
   &. ((review game)
            (separated fox man)
            (sameplace fox chicken)
            (disaster fox chicken))
   &. ((review game)
            (separated chicken man)
            (sameplace chicken grain)
            (disaster chicken grain))
   &. ((review game)
            (FORALL ((position-of X Y)) ((EQ Y right)))
            (PP) (PP Magic! You are a genius))
   &. ((review game) (PP) (PP OK so far) (PP))
   &. ((separated X Y)
            (NOT sameplace X Y))
```

&. ((sameplace X Y)
   (position-of X Z)
   (position-of Y Z))

&. ((disaster X Y)
   (DELCL ((position-of Y Z)))
   (PP) (PP DISASTER! X has eatern Y) (PP)
   (P New game? (enter 1 for yes, 0 for no):)
   (R x)
   (IF (EQ x 1)
      ((start y))
      ((ABORT))))

&. ((help X)
   (/* X is a throw-away argument)
   (PP) (PP These are the commands available)
   (PP)
   (PP start X)
   (PP load something)
   (PP get in)
   (PP row across)
   (PP get out)
   (PP unload something)
   (PP help me)
   (PP view X)
   (PP))

So much for the program clauses; now look at a possible use of them (but not necessarily one that will help you solve the puzzle successfully!):

&. start x ⟨ENTER⟩
&. load fox ⟨ENTER⟩
&. get in ⟨ENTER⟩

Once you have worked out the sequence of commands needed to solve this problem, you will probably notice that there are patterns of commands that get repeated.

Building those patterns into new commands that make typing out the solution quicker is stage two of the game. You might, for instance, like to define a new command (cross river) that combined the three actions needed to cross the river. You might also like to define a new command — perhaps calling it (take X) — combining the actions required to take something across the river. Finally, how about a command called (solve it), which does the whole thing in one fell swoop?

BLOCKSWORLD

Blocksworld is a classic microworld from the field of Artificial Intelligence research. Just as the turtle is linked with the name of Seymour Papert, so Blocksworld is linked with the name of Terry Winograd (see his book *Understanding Natural Language;* New York: Academic Press, 1972). The late Max Clowes wrote a cunningly-devised version in the computer language Pop-11, and it was at his feet that I made its acquaintance. The important thing to remember is that it is deliberately bugged: it does not do all that it is supposed to do, so that, in trying to make up the deficiencies, you will learn how the program works, and learn a good deal about computing into the bargain.

The basic scenario consists of a table and three blocks (in this version they are labelled c, g, and m, for cyan, green, and magenta). You are provided with three commands to enable you to move the blocks — (pickup X), (place(X Y)) and (letgo X) — and a number of others such as (start x), (view x), (data x), and (ch-size (X Y)). There is also (cls X) for setting the screen mode and colour: 'X' must be a legitimate colour-number, or (for the Sinclair Spectrum) 8 if you want to return from graphics mode to normal mode.

There are, however, some extras provided for you to work into the program. The three blocks are members of a structure called tower; and there are two other structures, one called stand, consisting of a block and a tub, and another called spire, consisting of a block and a triangle. You can easily change the contents of these structures if you wish.

On typing the command *start x,* you get the table and the tower on the screen. It is probably best then to practise using the three moving commands. When you are confident with those, try defining a new command (perhaps calling it *move*) that does those three in one. Once that works, try enriching it so that it can react intelligently when asked to move a block which is underneath another block.

You can then, if you wish, use *build* to put one of the other structures either on the table or on top of the tower. If you want to put something in the tub, you will have to modify the two commands *place* and *build.* If you want to *build* something on top of an individual block rather than a structure, you will have to modify *build* again. By all means define more blocks and other shapes: there is plenty of scope for experiment.

Here is a sample use of some of the commands in this version:

&. start x ⟨ENTER⟩
&. pickup g ⟨ENTER⟩
&. view x ⟨ENTER⟩
&. place(g table) ⟨ENTER⟩
&. data x ⟨ENTER⟩
&. letgo g ⟨ENTER⟩
&. view x ⟨ENTER⟩
&. build(stand table) ⟨ENTER⟩
&. view x ⟨ENTER⟩

You should also try picking up something that isn't there, and letting go of something before placing it anywhere. You might also like to explore the *ch-size* (= *change size*) command. If you like colour, you could explore filling the blocks with the colours of your choice. If you really want a challenge, convert the whole microworld from 2-D to 3-D.

Note that, apart from the command *build,* which can easily be modified by editing out the *view* command, the logical manipulations of the blocks are quite unconnected with their visual representation — you could do the whole thing without drawing anything on the screen, just using the (data x) command to keep you up to date with how things are going.

The program listing may be found in the Appendix. If you are typing it into your own computer, please take great care to distinguish between lower-case and capital letters. *By far the most common reason for a program not working is mis-typed variable names.*

6

Augmented turtle graphics

Turtle graphics originated with the computer language LOGO, and will always be associated with the name of Seymour Papert (see his inspiring book *Mindstorms*; Brighton: Harvestor Press, 1981). In recent years, they have been implemented in most computer languages, and they work very well in micro-PROLOG. The suggestions that follow are based on the turtle graphics and trigonometry modules listed in the Appendix. That means they are tailored for the Sinclair Spectrum, and will need some adaptation to work on other computers.

Squares
Assuming, then, that you have loaded the necessary modules, try typing in this little program:

&. ((sq X) (repeat 4 ((fd X) (tn 90)))) ⟨ENTER⟩

This will enable you to draw a square of any size; the 'X' can stand for any number. Remember, of course, that the screen of your TV or monitor can only cope with squares up to a certain limited size: after that, micro-PROLOG will signal

Error : 13

to show that you are trying to draw off the screen. So here is how you could use the *sq* program:

102 APPLICATIONS

    &. cls 7 ⟨ENTER⟩
    &. sq 50 ⟨ENTER⟩

cls

cls clears the screen to the colour of your choice — in the case above, Spectrum colour number 7 (white). The program also enables you to return from graphics mode to normal mode by typing

    &. cls 8 ⟨ENTER⟩

since for the Spectrum, 8 is not a colour number.

Pentagons, triangles, etc.

Once you have got the square program to work, try using it as a model for other shape programs. For example, write a program for a pentagon. The only things that will be different from the *sq* program will be (a) the name — perhaps *pent* instead of *sq*; (b) the number of repetitions — 5, not 4; and (c) the angle of turn. As you probably know, those last two numbers must multiply together to make 360. For a square, 4 * 90 = 360. For a five-sided figure (i.e. a pentagon), you need to work out 5 * ? = 360 to get the angle of turn.

When you have done a pentagon, see if you can do lots of other shapes with different numbers of sides. Watch out for the triangle: most people get that wrong the first time.

poly

You may already know that shapes like these where all the sides are the same length, are called 'regular polygons'. It would be a worthwhile achievement if we could write a single program that would do any regular polygon. It would have to work out for itself what angle of turn it had to use each time, but so long as we gave it the number of sides we wanted, it could do that quite easily. The only other thing it would need to know would be how long each side was to be. So we'll have to have two variables, one for the NUMBER of sides, and one for the LENGTH of each side.

```
    &. ((poly (X Y))
         (/* (X=no-of-sides)
             (Y=len-of-side)
             (Z-angle))
       (TIMES X Z 360)
       (repeat X ((fd Y) (tn Z)) )) ⟨ENTER⟩
```

And you could use it like this:

&. poly(4 40) ⟨ENTER⟩

or

&. poly(10 5) ⟨ENTER⟩

or

&. poly(7 20) ⟨ENTER⟩

With this last one — a heptagon — you may find that it doesn't meet up exactly at the end. This is because 360/7 does not give a whole-number answer, and this turtle only turns in whole-number steps.

face

I'd like to say two other things about the *poly* program. First, it sometimes works better if you get the turtle facing the top of the screen first: otherwise you may find you draw off the screen too easily. You can sort this out by using the *face* command. If you (face 90), the turtle will be pointing towards the top of the screen; (face 180) points it to the left-hand side; (face 270) points it to the bottom and (face 360) is the same as (face 0), pointing to the right. You can, of course, face any whole number between 0 and 360. So:

&. cls 7 ⟨ENTER⟩
&. face 90 ⟨ENTER⟩
&. poly(8 30) ⟨ENTER⟩

The second thing to say about *poly* is that you can use it to draw circles — or things that look very much like circles. This is possible if you do lots of repeats of lots of short sides, with only small turns in between each one.

&. cls 7 ⟨ENTER⟩
&. face 90 ⟨ENTER⟩
&. poly(36 10) ⟨ENTER⟩

This gives you a polygon of 36 sides, each side 10 units long — and it looks remarkably like a circle.

Rectangles

Now, what if we wanted to do shapes that did not have all their sides of equal length? A rectangle is a typical example. If you think about it, a rectangle still has two sides the same, so it is not that much different from a square:

&. ((rect (X Y))
        (repeat 2 ((fd X) (tn 90) (fd Y) (tn 90)))) ⟨ENTER⟩

which could be used like so:

&. cls 7 ⟨ENTER⟩
&. rect(10 20) ⟨ENTER⟩

Of course, if the two numbers you chose were the same as each other, you would get a square:

&. cls 7 ⟨ENTER⟩
&. rect(20 20) ⟨ENTER⟩

Circles

Although it is possible to draw 'circles' using the *poly* program, it is not particularly easy to visualize their size just from the number and length of their sides. It is easier to imagine the result if you actually have to choose the angle of turn directly — the bigger the angle, the tighter the circle. So here is a different circle program, which I find easier to use:

&. ((circle (X Y))
        (/∗ (X=len-of-side)
           (Y=angle)
           (Z=no-of-sides))
        (TIMES Y Z 360)
        (repeat Z ((fd X) (tn Y)))) ⟨ENTER⟩
&. cls 7 ⟨ENTER⟩
&. face 90 ⟨ENTER⟩
&. circle(10 10) ⟨ENTER⟩

Star

While we are on individual shapes, here is a program for a five-pointed star:

&. ((star X) (repeat 5 ((fd X) (tn 144)))) ⟨ENTER⟩

See if you can adapt this so as to draw a star with six points instead of five. Perhaps there is a program that will draw any star, just as there is for polygons.

Complex patterns

All these shapes so far are fairly simple, single figures. The fun starts when we build these simple programs into bigger ones, where whole shapes are repeated, with perhaps a turn in between each. Try this one:

&. ((pattern X) (repeat 20 ((sq X) (tn 10)))) ⟨ENTER⟩

&. cls 7 ⟨ENTER⟩

&. pattern 30 ⟨ENTER⟩

Try variations on this, for example with a pentagon or star instead of a square.

Another pleasing pattern is the spiral:

&. ((spiral X)
(make sidelength X)
(repeat 30 ((go-fwd) (tn 122) (increase-side-by 5))))

&. ((go-fwd) (sidelength X) (fd X))

&. ((increase-side-by X)
(sidelength Y)
(SUM X Y Z)
(make sidelength Z))

&. cls 7

&. spiral 5

This will make a triangular spiral. Try experimenting with different angles of turn so as to make, for example, a square spiral, or a hexagonal one. And later, when you have learnt how to use 'rem' (see p. 108ff), adapt this program to make a spiral whose coordinates will be remembered for use with the hare.

Artistic effects

There are a number of ways in which you can affect the look of your drawings. First of all, you do not have to be drawing all the time you are moving: you can tell the turtle to lift its pen up so that it is not touching the 'paper'. Then when it moves, it will leave no lines behind it. To restore drawing, you tell it to put its pen down to the 'paper' again. So.

&. pen up
&. fd 30
&. pen down
&. fd 10

should give you the idea of what is possible here.

Secondly, a more complicated version of *cls* enables you to do interesting things with the screen colouring. We have already seen that you can choose your screen colour: (cls 7) for white; (cls 5) for cyan; and so on, for the Spectrum.

With the Spectrum, you can control separately the colours of the background, the 'paper', and the 'ink'. So we have a command (cls X Y Z), where 'X' is the background colour, 'Y' the paper colour, and 'Z' the ink colour. Setting 'X' and 'Y' to the same colour, and 'Z' to a different one, gives standard high-resolution graphics. Setting 'X' to one colour, and 'Y' and 'Z' to the same colour as each other (but one that is different from 'X', of course), gives you a block graphics effect. You can set each to a different colour if you like, and see what happens. Here is how you give the commands:

&. ? ((cls 0 0 7)) ⟨ENTER⟩

for white lines on black paper. The only trouble here is that any commands that you type will also be in black, so you cannot tell what you are typing!

&. ? ((cls 2 2 7)) ⟨ENTER⟩

is a more practical choice.

&. ? ((cls 2 7 7)) ⟨ENTER⟩

gives you the bar graph effect.

&. ? ((cls 2 5 7)) ⟨ENTER⟩

is not very sharply defined, at least on the Spectrum.

Remember that (cls X) — that is, *cls* with one argument only — always sets the ink to black, and both the paper and background to whatever colour you enter for 'X'.

paper, ink

You can change the paper and ink colours independently at any time without clearing the screen, by using the separate *paper* and *ink* commands:

&. paper 2
&. ink 7

drto, jumpto
So far, we have only used what is technically called Euclidean Geometry (after the Greek mathematician Euclid); that is, we have dealt only with lines and angles. There is another branch of geometry known as Cartesian Geometry (after the French philosopher and mathematician Descartes), which goes in for (x, y) coordinates. Most computer screens are in fact controlled by programs that use (x, y) coordinates of some kind, so that using cartesian-geometry commands provides rather faster results than those we have used so far. Luckily, most versions of the turtle provide some such commands. In our version, there is (drto (X Y)) and (jumpto (X Y)).

To draw to a particular (x, y) coordinate, we use (drto (X Y)). (Note that we do not bother with the comma between the 'X' and the 'Y' in this version – it saves a deal of typing.) The nice thing about the cartesian method of drawing is that we do not have to worry about which way the turtle is facing.

(jumpto (X Y)), as you might expect, moves the turtle to your specified position without drawing a line – and you do not have to worry about whether the pen is up or down.

In fact, this turtle program uses (x, y) coordinates to keep track of where the turtle is anyway, even when you are doing lines and angles. You can see this from the data read-out that is produced by each command when you use it. We can therefore ask micro-PROLOG to make a note of each position the turtle stops at, so that we can use it later if we want to. In this way, we can save our drawings in a tape or disk file as a list of coordinates, and re-draw them any time. Moreover, re-drawing them will be very much faster than doing them first time around, because we can go straight to each coordinate instead of having to work out how long a line we need to draw to the next position, and what angle we need to turn to be facing the right way.

Nor is that all. With a list of coordinates to work with, we can easily achieve 'blow ups' or 'shrink downs' of our shapes, stretch them longways or sideways or both, flip them over on their sides or backs, and draw them in different places on the screen. This is called 'transformational geometry', since we are transforming our original shapes into new ones. To do all this, we simply need the little module listed as 'hare-mod' in the Appendix, and a couple of other commands in the original 'turt-mod' module.

rem, callit

If we want the computer to make a note of the coordinates the turtle stops at, we add (rem x) to the program:

&. ((square X) (repeat 4 ((fd X) (tn 90) (rem X)))) ⟨ENTER⟩

The 'X' in (rem X) is actually a throw-away argument in case you want to use *rem* as a separate command outside a program; for example, when you are drawing a complicated shape with single *fd* and *tn* commands, and where some trial and error is involved:

&. cls 7
&. fd 10
&. rem x
&. tn 135
&. fd 40
&. rem x
&. face 270
&. fd 100
&. bk 10
&. rem x

Here, the (fd 100) command was not quite what I wanted, so before getting micro-PROLOG to remember the coordinates, I told the turtle to go back 10 units.

What (rem x) actually does is to add to the computer's memory a clause of the form (coord (X Y)) each time it is used.

When my drawing is finished, I tell micro-PROLOG to gather up all the individual coordinates it has been noting down, and put them into a single list together with a name for that drawing. To do this, I use the command *callit*. So if I wanted to use the *square* program above, I could do this:

&. cls 7
&. square 20
&. callit box

This will produce a clause

((coords box ((20 0) (20 20) (0 20) (0 0))))

in the computer's memory, at the same time deleting each (coord (X Y)) clause.

Note that *cls* KILLs any individual (coord (X Y)) clauses left over from a previous session, so that you start with a clean sheet. However, it will not interfere with anything you have assembled using *callit.*

The hare
We are now in a position to use the facilities of the hare — so-called because it is a fast companion for the turtle.

The basic hare command is *show,* and it works just like the *which* command in the database chapter, except that it plots the result of its computation instead of writing it out in words. So

&. cls 7
&. show(X (coords box X))

will take each coordinate in the list 'X' and join it to the next with a line — very fast.

To make use of the transformational abilities of the hare, you use *rotate* and *mod* (= 'modify'). Here are some examples:

&. cls 7
&. show(X (coords box Y) (rotate Y 45 X))

This says 'show X such that the coordinates of box are Y, and Y rotated by 45 degrees yields list X'.

&. cls 7
&. show(X (coords box Y) (mod Y times (2 1) X))

Here, each x-coordinate of the original list of coordinates 'Y' is multiplied by 2, while each y-coordinate is multiplied by 1, to give a new list 'X'; that is then plotted by *show.* So we get a version of *box* that is stretched horizontally by a factor of 2.

&. cls 7
&. show (X (coords box Y)
   (mod Y times (2 2) Z)
   (mod Z sum (60 0) X))

Now *box* is first doubled in size, then shifted to the new location (60 0) by adding 60 to each x-coordinate and 0 to each y-coordinate.

Suppose that we wrote a new *pattern* program for the turtle, this time using *square* instead of *sq* (so that (rem x) was included in its definition). That would cause each coordinate to be remembered by the computer as it drew it.

&. ((pattern2 X) (repeat 20 ((square X) (tn 10))))

&. cls 7
&. pattern2 20
&. callit clam

We could now have fun using *clam* with the hare:

&. show(X (coords clam X))
&. show(X (coords clam Y)
          (mod Y sum (−60 0) X))
&. show(X (coords clam Y)
          (mod Y times (−1 1) Z)
          (mod Z sum (60 0) X))

Try changing the colours, too. White ink on red paper is quite effective.

plot

It is worth noting that the *show* command is defined as follows:

&. ((show (X | Y))
        (? Y)
        (plot X))

That command *plot* is also available to you separately if you want it.

DESIGNING YOUR OWN ALPHABET

One thing you can do with the turtle is design an alphabet of your own. You can choose the typeface and size, and indeed the nationality. A simple way to begin is to define certain types of line — vertical, horizontal, sloping — which can then be used to build up whole letters. Once again, I am indebted to Marcus Gray and Michael Coker from whose Pop-11 programs this is adapted.

&. ((vertical (X Y))
        (face 90)
        (from X Y 10))

&. ((horizontal (X Y))
        (face 0)
        (from X Y 10))

&. ((sloping (X Y))
    (face 60)
    (from X Y 10))

&. ((from X Y Z)
    (jumpto (X Y))
    (fd Z))

With these, you could perhaps make a letter 'C':

&. ((C (X Y))
    (horizontal (X Y))
    (vertical (X Y))
    (SUM Y 10 Z)
    (horizontal (X Z)))

In each case, the (X Y) is the point on the screen at which you wish drawing to start. See if you can define the rest of the alphabet. You will need some other types of line besides the three given above.

The real challenge, of course, is to design a non-Roman alphabet — Greek, Russian, Hindustani, Hebrew, Arabic, Japanese. Be bold! Have a go!

7

Databases

A database is simply a collection of information, or data, about some topic or other. Computers are very good for storing and gaining access to such collections, because storage is compact, and access is very fast — *if* you have an intelligent program to sort through the data for you. Both such tasks suit micro-PROLOG down to the ground. In this chapter, we shall discuss three of the modules listed in the Appendix: 'expert-mod', and the pair 'dbase-mod' and 'rules-mod'.

'expert-mod' sets up a so-called expert-system, which is one way of organizing a database. As its name implies, an expert-system claims to be an expert on a particular subject. You consult it as a client when you have questions about that subject, and it either leads you through the data in a controlled fashion to an answer, or, if it cannot work out the answer, it asks to be informed of it so that it can store it away for future reference. This means that you can use the module to build up your database from scratch as well as to question it.

If the expert does succeed in answering your question, it is also capable of explaining how it arrived at its answer, and why the answer is not something else: that is, you can ask 'why so' and 'why-not something-else' (where 'something-else' is a specific, named item, e.g. 'why-not leopard' in the case of an expert-system on animal identification).

Very often, however, it is quite unnecessary to go the trouble of setting up an expert system to handle your data. If your are just organizing the computer equivalent of a card-file on your personal library, for instance, you want something much more simple. 'dbase-mod' and 'rules-mod' are designed to assist you in setting up well-organized databases, and in writing the rules that you will need to teach the computer for it to access the data in the way you want it to. They also offer general-purpose questioning-commands, or 'querying commands' as they are more usually known, which help to make the rules you define effective and powerful.

AN EXPERT SYSTEM

This expert system does three things. (1) It answers your questions if it can. (2) It can ask for and remember new information. (3) It can have a go at justifying its answer. It is designed to cope with any category of data, but we shall take all our examples from one category for the sake of coherence: we shall stick to animals, since using the system to play the animal identification game provides a good demonstration of its capabilities.

Answering your questions

Imagine that you are asking the computer to guess what animal you are thinking of. You would type

    &. name animal ⟨ENTER⟩

Two commands are offered at the top level: *diagnose* and *name*. *diagnose* seems more appropriate when the system is being used for fault-finding or sickness diagnosis, while *name* seems more appropriate for animal identification or library access. You could easily define other synonyms such as *find*:

    &. ((find X) (diagnose X))

Here are the definitions of *name* and *diagnose*. Please note, by the way, that we shall not be listing and examining here every cluase in the definition of 'expert-mod': only enough to enable you to see what is going on.

```
    ((name X) (diagnose X))      /* name is a synonym for diagnose
    ((diagnose X)                /* X is a category-name, e.g. "animal"
        (clear X)                /* Prepare for new consultation
        (CL ((X | Y) | Z))       /* Get a clause of relevant category;
```

(check-out X Y Z)) /∗ Check it out.
((diagnose X) /∗ If it doesn't check out, ask
(learn-about X)) /∗ to learn about it.

When you use this, 'X' must be a category, such as 'animal', or 'book', and *not* an example within a category – 'lion', or 'Treasure Island'.

At this point, let us look at the sort of data these clauses would be dealing with.

&. ((animal lion)
(lives in Africa)
(cat family)
(golden coloured))
&. ((animal polar bear)
(lives in America)
(eats meat)
(eats fish)
(very big and heavy)
(has all-white fur))

In the definition of lion, 'cat family' implies several other characteristics, so we would need to define those, too:

&. ((implies (eats meat) (cat family)))
&. ((implies (has four legs) (cat family)))

Returning now to the expert system, *check-out* and its sub-clauses are defined like this:

((check-out X Y Z) /∗ X is the category, Y the example,
 e.g. lion,
(! check Z) /∗ Z the defining characteristics of lion
(consultation X Y Z))

((check X)
(FORALL ((true Y)) ((test Y X)))
(FORALL ((false Y)) ((NOT test Y X))))

((test X Y)
(OR ((member X Y)) ((implied-in X Y))))

((implied-in X Y) /∗ X is implied in list-of-symptoms Y if
(implies X Z) /∗ Z is noted as implying X, and
(member Z Y)) /∗ Z occurs in list Y.

The point of having a *check* clause at all is to eliminate wasteful duplication of questions to the user by the computer. Many animals will have similar characteristics (e.g. both lion and tiger are members of the cat family), so if you have already answered the question whether or not the animal you are thinking of is a member of the cat family, then you do not want to have to answer it again. As you will see from the definition of *consultation,* the computer makes a note of each answer you give it, and checks later queries against those before asking you anything.

If nothing in the *check* clauses makes the expert discard the specification it is currently examining, it then proceeds to ask you about each characteristic in the specification list that it does not already know about. For example, it will ask you whether your animal lives in Africa. If you say yes, it will go on to the next characteristic, and ask about that. If you say no, it will reject the whole list of characteristics, backtrack to the *diagnose* clause, and get another list (or, if there are no more, will ask you what your were thinking of).

If it has worked right through a list of characteristics and not had cause to discard it, it will offer the 'owner' of those characteristics (perhaps 'lion') as the answer to your question. (Incidentally, in the program notes below, 'symptom' is used instead of 'characteristic', because it is shorter.)

```
((consultation X Y ())          /* IF the symptom list is empty
    (PP Your X appears to be)   /* and therefore finished, offer
    (P " " | Y)                 /* the answer.
    (PP))
((consultation X Y (Z | x))     /* ELSE IF we take the next
                                       symptom,
    (true Z)                    /* and it is already noted as
                                       true,
    (consultation X Y x))       /* proceed with next symptom.
((consultation X Y (Z | x))     /* ELSE, if next symptom not
    (NOT true Z)                /* noted as true, get user to
    (relevance Z y)             /* show its relevance,
    (IF (EQ y 1)                /* IF relevance "1", then
        ((add true Z)           /* note Z as true,
        (consultation X Y x))   /* go on to next symptom.
```

```
            ((IF (EQ y 0)        /* ELSE IF relevance "0", then
                ((add false Z)   /* note Z as false,
                FAIL)            /* backtrack.
                ((consultation X Y (Z | x)))  /* ELSE, go round
                                                 again
            ))                   /* unchanged if
                                    relevance
        )                        /* not "1" or "0".
    )
)
```

Explaining *why* **and** *why-not*

Some people trust computers not at all; others take their output as gospel. The best attitutde is much like that appropriate to the human expert: guarded trust, perhaps, but fundamentally a fierce attachment to one's own common sense. We must, therefore, be able to find out why a computer reaches a given decision. This system offers (somewhat crude) *why* and *why-not* facilities, based on the inventory of things you have indicated as being true or false. The *why* command just reads back to you a list of what you have said was true or false. The *why-not* command compares those true and false items with the specification of the alternative which you have named, and returns with a list of the discrepancies. If your alternative is not in the database, the system again seeks to be informed.

```
((why X)
    (PP Because you said the following were true)
    (show true)
    (PP)
    (PP And because you said the following were false)
    (show false))

((why-not X)
    (category Y)           /* Remind myself what
                              category is in view,
    (to-list X Z)          /* make sure requested
                              example is in list form;
    (IF (CL ((Y | Z) | x)) /* IF the example is in the
                              database,
```

```
        ((compare Z x))       /* compare Z-and-x with true/
                                 false statements;
        ((clear Y)            /* ELSE clear decks to add to
                                 knowledge of Y:
        (add-spec Y X)) ))    /* add specification of X to
                                 database.
```

A more sophisticated expert-system should let you ask *why* at any stage of the consultation, in case you cannot see the purpose of a particular question. The explanatory aspect of expert systems is an important focus of research.

Learning new information

Rather than simply giving up if it fails to find an answer to your query, the expert actively seeks to fill this gap in its knowledge: it uses *learn-about* and *ask-about* to see if you can teach it.

```
   ((learn-about X)
        (CLS 7)              /* Clear the screen; white background
        (PP I'm afraid I can't help you)
        (ask-about X))

   ((ask-about X)
        (get-answer Y)       /* Get the answer Y
        (add-spec X Y))      /* and the specification of Y from
                             /* you, and add it to the database.
```

In assembling the specification for the new item, the expert makes use of any *true* clauses noted as a result of the foregoing consultation. These are displayed, and you are asked to add whatever other characteristics are necessary to define your animal adequately. Thus if the animal you were thinking of was 'skunk', and the system only knew about 'lion' and 'polar bear' as defined above, the following *true* clause should be in the database after the consultation stage:

    ((true (lives in America))

The expert tells you:

    I know the following about skunk:

        (lives in America)

    Please add characteristics one at a time IN BRACKETS

You then type in such things as

    (has four legs)
    (raids dustbins)
    (makes delightful smells)
    (striped white from nose to tail)
    0

The zero indicates that you have finished describing your animal.

All this means that you can build a database from scratch just by starting with your 'expert-mod' and no data, choosing your category — let's choose *book* for now — and typing

    &. name book ⟨ENTER⟩

Since there would be no data about *book* in the computer, the expert would have to resort to asking you for information about book:

    Sorry, I can't help you: please tell me the answer

You would then give the specification of your first book.

To add information about your second and subsequent books, your could use *why-not*. Suppose your second book was *Gone With The Wind*, you would type

    &. why-not (Gone With The Wind) ⟨ENTER⟩

The expert would then ask you to give it the 'characteristics' of *Gone With The Wind*, and add your description to its database.

One of the advantages of an expert-system such as this is that it is not important to the expert how many characteristics a particular animal or book has. In the second half of this chapter, we shall look at a more common format for databases, where each entry must have exactly the same number of 'characteristics', or 'fields', as the next, and where the fields must be in the same order for each entry.

TOOLS FOR DATABASES

Let us now consider 'dbase-mod' and 'rules-mod', as listed in the Appendix. They are designed to help you plan, set up, and query a typical database. 'What is a typical database?', I hear you ask. Let us settle on a representative topic, and follow some examples right through.

We shall take as our model a booklist cross-indexed by topic so that it forms an index of resources on a range of subjects. We shall decide that each entry will take the general form

((book title)
    (author)
    (publisher)
    (topics covered))

A specific example would be

((book Robinson Crusoe)
    (Defoe D)
    (Desert Island Books Ltd)
    (shipwreck desert-islands Friday))

The point is that in this database, the title is *always* the first 'characteristic' of the book to be listed, the author is *always* the second, and so on; in this way we do not have to put the word 'author' in as well as 'Defoe D.'. This contrasts with a database where you do put in words like 'author' as well as the person's actual name, and which therefore allows you to vary the order in which you make your entries. The expert-system described above assembles its database in that sort of way. The type of database we describe here is more economical but less flexible.

The regularly-placed characteristics of our database are called 'fields'. So the first field is the title field, the second is the author field, the third the publisher field, and the fourth the topics field. 'dbase-mod' will in fact require you to name the fields that you want for any particular database, and will use those names, and the order in which you typed them, as its template for setting up the data you then give it.

Note also that each of our *book* entries will have the SAME NUMBER of characteristics. Again, the expert-system would allow us to have, say, two characteristics for one entry, four for another, three for another, and so on. So these are two quite different ways of going about using the computer to store information.

Building the database: 'dbase-mod'
Each time you want to add information to the database, you use the

name of the category — in this chapter we are using *book* — and the command *add,* thus:

&. add book ⟨ENTER⟩

The program immediately adds to the memory (if it does not already contain it) the clause

((category book))

The first time you use *add* for any category, 'dbase-mod' will ask you to give it the names of the fields you want it to store the information in:

Please type name of first field

It will continue to ask you for field-names until you type a zero to indicate the end of that stage of the exercise. The program then adds to the memory a clause of this type:

((fields book (title author publisher topics)))

So you must plan your fields before entering any data.

Once it has the field-names, 'dbase-mod' will allow you to enter some information. It will print the name of the first field on the screen, and ask you to say what you wish to go into that slot of your first entry. In our example, we decided to have 'title' as our first field, so we would see on the screen

Now type in title IN BRACKETS

Each of the fields would be presented in turn in the same manner, until the program had worked through its field-list. If we had typed in that our title was (Treasure Island), our author (Stevenson R L), our publisher (Adventure Books Ltd.), and our topics (treasure sailing parrots one-legged-men), the program would add to the memory the following clause:

((book Treasure Island)
        (Stevenson R L)
        (Adventure Books Ltd.)
        (treasure sailing parrots one-legged-men))

You could now do one of two things: you could use *add* again to enter information about your next book, or you could leave that for the moment and turn to making your rules of access to the data. I strongly recommend that you do the latter, because it is just possible that in making up the rules, you will decide that you have left out some vital field of information, or that you want the data organized in some rather different way. It is no trouble doing this if you only have one entry in your database: it is a wretched nuisance if you have lots.

Writing rules of access: 'rules-mod'
So we shall turn now to 'rules-mod'. This module offers only one command: *rules-for,* and you use it like this:

&. rules-for book ⟨ENTER⟩

You will then be presented with the list of field-names that you had previously given the computer, and instructions about the format of any rule you may wish to teach the computer.

A query of the book information we are discussing might say 'Give me the author of the book entitled Treasure Island'; or 'Give me all the books by Stevenson R. L.'; or 'Give me all the books about one-legged-men'. Such queries would need micro-PROLOG rules that looked like this:

((author-of X Y) (/∗ X=title Y=author) . . .

and

((topics X Y) (/∗ X=title Y=topics) . . .

The parts of the rules indicated by '. . .' can easily be written for you by the computer, saving you making typing and other sorts of errors, and that is what 'rules-mod' does for you. There is, of course, nothing to stop you looking at the rules, once 'rules-mod' has defined them for you, studying how they work, and then trying to write your own versions. In fact, that is one of the reasons for adopting this approach. So be curious: explore and tinker.

Returning, then, to the actual process of giving 'rules-mod' the rule you want, you will have to type in this sort of thing:

(author-of title author)

and

(topics title topics)

The program will then use the first word in each list as a label, or relation-name, for its rule, and the second and third words as indications of which fields are to be investigated by this rule. Once again, you type in a zero when you have finished giving your rules. Two things then happen. First, 'rules-mod' adds to the memory clauses of the type

 ((rules author-of))

and

 ((rules topics))

so that you can remind yourself at a later date what rules are available with this database by typing

 &. LIST rules ⟨ENTER⟩

And second, the completely-defined rules are now added to the memory and LISTed on the screen for you to see. You should then test them (see next section). If they work, you can

 &. KILL rules-mod ⟨ENTER⟩

to give yourself more free memory.

Querying the data: 'dbase-mod' again

'dbase-mod' provides a powerful command called *which* to help you use your rules effectively. As they stand, the rules only give you *one* answer to any question; *which* arranges for them to keep working until they have given you all possible answers to any particular request. Thus to get an answer to the question posed above – 'Give me all the books by Stevenson R L' – you would type this:

 &. which (X (author-of X (Stevenson R L)) ⟨ENTER⟩

The first argument of *which* must indicate the variables whose values you want printed out. If there is more than one of them, then you must bracket them together so that they still form a single argument:

 &. which((X Y) (author-of X Y)) ⟨ENTER⟩

Here we have asked for the names of all the books together with their authors.

We can in fact ask for text to be included in the reply from the computer:

&. which((X: by Y) (author-of X Y)) ⟨ENTER⟩

The response would now come back in the form

(Treasure Island) : by (Stevenson R L)

We can also string multiple requests together:

&. which((X Y Z) (author-of X Y) (topics X Z)) ⟨ENTER⟩

and

&. which((X Y)
         (author-of (Treasure Island) X)
         (publisher (Treasure Island) Y)) ⟨ENTER⟩

and

&. which((X Y)
         (author-of X Y)
         (topics X Z)
         (member one-legged-men Z)) ⟨ENTER⟩

The rule *member* is already defined for you inside 'dbase-mod', so you do not have to worry about writing it yourself.

Additional facilities of 'dbase-mod'
delete
There will probably come a time when you want to edit your database. One thing that happens is that an entry is no longer needed. You can get rid of individual entries by using *delete* together with the information in the first field of the entry. In the case of *book* that would be information about a title. Thus

&. delete (Treasure Island) ⟨ENTER⟩

would get rid of all the information on that book in your database.

edit
There is also a little editor that works in the same way, i.e. by reference to the information in the first field of an entry, so that you could say

&. edit (Treasure Island) ⟨ENTER⟩

Writing rules by yourself

'rules-mod' only allows you to write rules with two arguments, but there are many other types of rules that you might want to write. In particular, you might want to bypass *which* and write special-purpose rules that printed all answers instead of just one. Let's look at one or two examples of such work. In each case, they will make use of the rules written by 'rules-mod'.

The data on books that we have set up has all the topics for each entry packaged together in one list, but invariably one wants to access the data according to a single topic. So our first hand-made rule will enable us to get all books on a given single topic:

&. ((topic X)
  (PP)
  (FORALL ((topics Y Z) (member X Z))
    ((PP | Y))))

and you could use that thus:

&. topic one-legged-men ⟨ENTER⟩

A similar rule would produce all the books by a given author:

&. ((author X)
  (PP)
  (FORALL ((author-of Y X))
    ((PP | Y))))

Usage for that would be

&. author (Stevenson R L) ⟨ENTER⟩

A different style for your data

The format adopted by 'dbase-mod' for your data involves putting several lists inside the one basic micro-PROLOG list, but you do not have to do it that way. The in some ways simpler alternative is to put all the information inside one list only, like this:

((book (Treasure Island) (Stevenson R L) (Adventure Books Ltd.)
  (pirates . . .)))

which could then be referred to as

    (book | X)

instead of the rather more complicated

    (CL ((book | X) | Y)

that the format adopted by 'dbase-mod' requires. I adopted the more complicated style for 'dbase-mod' because when you come to LIST your information, it is much easier to read in the clausal form than in the single-list form.

There is one other style that could be adopted:

((book ((Treasure Island) (Stevenson R L) (Adventure Books Ltd.)

    (pirates . . .))))

and that could be referred to as

    (book X)

Which format you choose is up to you: it makes little difference to micro-PROLOG.

SUMMARY

This chapter, then, has attempted to give you an introduction to expert-systems, to databases in different formats, and to the business of writing rules of access to such databases. micro-PROLOG is a fast and flexible language for this kind of application, and once you have got the idea of the formalisms and strategies involved, you should be able to have fun developing your own databases in your own style.

8

Natural language

In this chapter we shall look at the ideas involved in constructing a simple sentence generator, and then expand that to include the beginnings of an automatic language translator.

A SENTENCE GENERATOR
Introduction
In constructing this sentence generator, there will be a number of intermediate programs as the ideas are worked out, leading to a final program that is fast and powerful. By that time I hope you will have the tools to take this kind of activity further if you wish.

The possibilities for foreign language-teaching
As will be obvious when we progress to translation, there is no reason to confine this sort of work to your native language. It can be the basis for some exciting foreign language-teaching, and I hope that this is one direction readers will wish to strike off in. It is worth saying in this connection that the great attraction of this exercise to students is the opportunity to include all sorts of wild vocabulary, and to see it come out in even wilder combinations; so the teacher risks killing the fun of it if he or she imposes censorship.

Preparing a tool-kit

The basis of a sentence-generator is a sequence of PROLOG rules that take the building blocks of sentences, namely, words, and strings them together according to the relevant grammatical rules.

Introducing modern grammar

There are many models of English grammar, but without prejudice we shall settle on one to illustrate our generator.

We shall assume that all English sentences can be split into two parts — a noun phrase (NP) and a verb phrase (VP). Here are a few examples:

	NP	VP
1.	Birds	fly
2.	Pilots	fly aeroplanes
3.	The worm	turns
4.	The early bird	catches the worm
5.	The very cunning bird	catches the worm with a mousetrap

As you can see, there are several possible varieties of NP, and similarly with the VP. An NP may consist of just a noun (1 and 2); or a noun and an article (which linguists now call a 'determiner', and we shall call 'det' for short) (3); or there can be an adjective as well (4); or even an adverb and an adjective (5).

The VP may likewise consist of just a verb (1 and 3); or a verb and an NP (2 and 4); or a verb, an NP, and something else which, for the sake of argument, we shall call an adverb phrase (AdvP).

None of this is exhaustive; it is merely to give you the rough idea. A linguist would lay out these rules in the following sort of fashion (the arrow '→' means 'may consist of'):

S → NP VP
NP → noun
NP → det noun
NP → det AdjP noun

VP → verb
VP → verb NP
VP → verb NP AdvP

AdjP → adj
AdjP → adv adj

AdvP → adv
AdvP → prep NP

noun → birds
noun → pilots
... etc.
verb → fly
... etc.
det → the
... etc. etc. etc.

Grammar rules in PROLOG

Our task now is to express these grammar rules in micro-PROLOG. The most efficient formula is rather complex, so we shall construct a grammar-building kit which will add the necessary complications for us. Our grammar rules may also turn out to be complex, so let's build into our tool-kit the capability to include REMARKS (using the '/*' built-in symbol) and other useful system (i.e. built-in) commands such as NOT and EQ. I shall also assume the kit is all wrapped up as a module, so that we can kill off our first, primitive grammars and develop more sophisticated ones, yet keep our grammar-building kit intact (for a complete listing, see the Appendix).

A grammar-building tool-kit

There are three parts to this tool-kit. First is a facility for adding grammar rules to the database. Second, a similar facility for adding vocabulary. And third, the formula for screen display of the sentences that will be generated.

Adding grammar rules

To help add grammar rules, we shall provide a tool consisting of the following group of clauses:

&. ((rule X) (rulex X Y) (ADDCL Y))
&. ((rulex ((X | Y) | Z) ((X (X x) y | Y) | z))
      (body Z (x y) z))
&. ((body ((X | Y) (Z | x)) (y z) ((X y z | Y) (Z | x)))
      (SYS Z))
&. ((body ((X | Y)) (Z x) ((X Z x | Y))))

&. ((body ((X | Y) | Z) x ((X | Y) | y))
    (SYS X)
    (body Z x y))
&. ((body ((X | Y) | Z) (x y) ((X x z | Y) | X1))
    (body Z (z y) X1))

An example usage comes after we have seen how to add vocabulary.

Adding vocabulary

We provide a similar but simpler tool for adding vocabulary:

&. ((vocab ((X Y | Z) | x))
    (caps Y y)
    (ADDCL ((X (X y | z) z | Z) | x)))
&. ((caps X Y)
    (STRINGOF Z X)
    (to-caps Z x)
    (STRINGOF x Y))
&. ((caps X X))
&. ((to-caps () ()))
&. ((to-caps (X | Y) (Z | x))
    (IF (between a "z" X)
        ((capital X Z))
        ((EQ X Z)))
    (to-caps Y x))
&. ((between X Y Z)
    (NOT LESS Z X)
    (NOT LESS Y Z))
&. ((capital X Y)
    (CHAROF X Z)
    (SUM x 32 Z)
    (CHAROF Y x))

This makes sure, among other things, that all your actual words are in capitals, while your grammatical categories stay in lower case (assuming you type them in lower case to start with).

A very simple grammar program
We now have the tools with which to construct very powerful grammars, but let's start simply.

&. rule((sent) (np) (vp))
&. vocab((np (The red and white striped paint)))
&. vocab((vp (spilled out of the can)))

To generate a sentence using these data, we could type

&. ?((sent x( )) (PP x))

This is a crude way to do it, and is improved on below when we define *generate,* but it requires no further preparation.

We have here, then, the wherewithal to get a session going quickly (assuming you have prepared your tool-kit in advance), with scope for lots of zaney vocabulary combinations. The next stage is to diversify the grammar.

Clearing the decks
When starting on a new grammar, you obviously have to clear out the old one. This requires us to KILL some of the programs that we have entered. If our tool-kit is wrapped up as a module (see the Appendix for the listing), we simply type

&. KILL ALL

Otherwise we must be selective, for example:

&. KILL (sent np vp)

Extending the grammar – stage 1
Our first effort at improvement concerns different types of NP and VP:

&. rule((sent) (np) (vp))

&. rule((np) (noun))
&. rule((np) (det) (noun))
&. rule((np) (det) (adjp) (noun))

&. rule((vp) (verb))
&. rule((vp) (verb) (np))
&. rule((vp) (verb) (np) (advp))

&. rule((adjp) (adj))
&. rule((adjp) (adv) (adj))
&. rule((advp) (adv))
&. rule((advp) (prep) (np))
&. vocab((det the))
&. vocab((noun bat))
&. vocab((noun blood))
&. vocab((noun belfry))
&. vocab((verb sucks))
&. vocab((prep in))
&. vocab((adj black))
&. vocab((adv greedily))

One of the mistakes to watch for is inconsistency between abbreviations (such as *vb*) and full words (such as *verb*). I often find that I have typed *vb* in the body of a vp rule, but *verb* at the head of the vocabulary item (or *vice versa*). The computer won't match *vb* with *verb*, unless you program it do do so.

Screen display
Different people will want to bring out different aspects of this exercise in the display process. Here is just one way you could do it ('sp' stands for 'sentence print'):

&. ((sp (sent (np X vp Y)))
   (spr X Y))
&. ((sp (sent (np X)))
   (append Y (vp Z) X)
   (spr X Y))
&. ((spr X Y)
   (PP)
   (PP NP X)
   (PP VP Y))
&. ((append ( ) X X))
&. ((append (X | Y) Z (X | x))
   (append Y Z x))
&. ((generate X)
   (FORALL ((sent X ( ) | Y)) ((sp X))))

This is used by typing

&. generate x

It might be worth commenting here on the program *append*. *append* takes its first two arguments (which must be lists) and joins them together to make its third argument. But it can also take its third argument (which must be a list again) and split it apart in any way you define, to give two sublists as its first and second arguments. In the *sp* program above, it is doing the latter.

Extending the grammar – stage 2
So far, we have no means of checking Number agreement (singular noun with singular verb, for example) and all the other types of agreement that good grammars should have. Using out tool-kit, however, it is easy to extend the ideas in our basic grammar to include this kind of checking. The principle is, to add extra arguments, when specifying our rules and vocabulary, to provide for the matching of each particular type of agreement that we want to cover. Here is a brief indicator (we'd need to kill off all our old grammar again):

&. rule((sent) (np x) (vp x) (/* (x is number)))

&. vocab((np birds plural))
&. vocab((vp fly plural))
&. vocab((vp flies sing))

Now our sentence rule would not accept (birds flies) as a possibility, because in the *sent* rule, the argument of np has to match the argument of vp, and our vocabulary specification has ensured that that match is not present in the case of 'birds plural' and 'flies sing'.

Let's take this one stage further, though, since it will help us to learn by a contrasting case. KILL your old rules again, then try this:

&. rule((sent) (np x) (vp x) (/* (x is number))
&. rule((np x) (noun x))
&. rule((vp x) (verb x))
&. rule((vp x) (verb x) (np y))

&. vocab((noun birds pl))
&. vocab((verb eat pl))
&. vocab((noun fruit sing))

The point here is that, although the SUBJECT NP must agree with the verb in number, the OBJECT NP does *not* have to do so: we can have a plural verb followed by a singular noun as in 'eat fruit'. Therefore, we must distinguish carefully between the two arguments that must match (as in the *sent* rule, where both 'np' and 'vp' have the argument 'x'), and the argument of the object NP which does not have to match (where we have written a different variable 'y').

Adding person checking
If you have grasped the principle involved in Number checking, you should have little trouble in appreciating that we can simply add another argument that has to be matched for Person checking. Thus:

&. KILL ALL
&. rule((sent) (np x y) (vp x y) (/∗ (x person) (y number)))
&. rule((np x y) (pronoun x y))
&. rule((vp x y) (verb x y))

&. vocab((pronoun I 1 sing))
&. vocab((pronoun you 2 x))
&. vocab((pronoun he 3 sing))
&. vocab((verb eats 3 sing))
&. vocab((verb eat 1 sing))
... etc.

Adding gender-checking; an example from French

&. rule((sent) (np x y z) (vp x y z) (/∗ (x person) (y num)
    (z gender)))
&. rule((np x y z) (pronoun x y z))
&. rule((vp x y z) (verb x y z))

&. vocab((pronoun je 1 sing x))
&. vocab((pronoun tu 2 sing x))
&. vocab((pronoun il 3 sing m))
&. vocab((pronoun elle 3 sing f))
... etc.

I hope that those interested in languages other than English will begin to see how this sort of sentence-generating exercise can be of use in teaching and learning any language. And may I emphasize that for the pupil the fun comes when free rein is given to the imagination and vocabulary.

In the next section, we shall be using the ideas developed here as the basis for some computer language translation programs.

Making a module
As mentioned earlier, the grammar kit cries out to be a module, so that different grammars can be KILLed off while the tool-kit is preserved intact. The details of 'gram-mod' may be found in the Appendix.

Changing the display format
You may find that you do not like the way sentences are displayed by these programs, since each word is labelled according to the grammatical category it has been analyzed as filling. Some people who have used the programs preferred just the plain text. If you find yourself in the same boat, it is very simple to edit things so as to eliminate grammatical labels. First, open the module with

&. OPMOD gram-mod

Then call the editor to change *rulex* (i.e. the little editor described in the modules chapter); N.B. The editor cannot be loaded while gram-mod is open

&. ed rulex 1

and change it so that it ends up looking like this:

&. ((rulex ((X | Y) | Z) ((X x y | Y) | z))
    (body Z (x y) z))

Now edit *vocab*

&. ed vocab 1

so that it looks like this:

((vocab((X Y | Z) | x)
   (caps Y y)
     (ADDCL((X x | y) y | Z)))

Finally, edit *generate*

&. ed generate 1

so that it looks like this

&. ((generate X)
       (FORALL ((sent X () | Y)) ((PP) (PP | X))))

COMPUTER LANGUAGE TRANSLATION

Introduction
Human translators command good salaries or, to put it another way, they are expensive. Institutions that require large numbers of them, such as the U.N. and the E.E.C., are therefore particularly interested in computer language translation. Indeed, a fair amount of it already happens. It will be well worth our while, therefore, to look at what is involved and attempt some low-level translation ourselves. We are lucky in that micro-PROLOG must be one of the best computer languages available for this sort of work.

Broad outline
We shall need, first of all, to be able to analyze a sentence of input so as to capture the necessary degree of grammatical specification; and second, to take that specification and use it to generate an acceptable sentence in the target language. Obviously, then, our grammatical specification must be general enough to be applicable to more than one language – no easy task, I can assure you! And I should be frank at the outset and warn you that even those computer language translators in commercial use are imperfect. 'All grammars leak', said Chomsky. Ours will certainly do that, but it will serve to illustrate some of the basic ideas.

Stage one: the Noun Phrase
Let us settle on English and French as the languages between which to translate. And let us aim first to deal with such sentences as

(1) The man likes the woman – L'homme aime la femme
(2) The men like the women – Les hommes aiment les femmes
(3) I like her – Je l'aime

How do the English and the French compare? Well, for a start, the French equivalent of 'the' varies with the gender of the noun it precedes – 'la' before 'femme', 'le' cut down to 'l'' before 'homme' – unlike the English 'the'. So we must provide for the idea of Gender.

Similarly, we must provide for the idea of Number (i.e. singular or plural), since French not only has 'le' and 'la', but 'les' also. Finally, from the fact that verbs in both languages vary according to the Person of the subject — in English we have 'he likes' but 'I like', and in French we have 'aime', 'aimes', 'aimons', 'aimez', and 'aiment' — it is obvious that the category of Person must be included in our specification. So, PERSON, NUMBER, GENDER; and that is just the beginning! Incidentally, we shall refer to these three as 'png' for short.

Four other essentials must be noted. We need to mark each word for the language to which it belongs. We also need some sort of base-meaning word or 'root' to enable us to switch from one language to the other and still keep the sense. This marker could be a unique number for the particular word, or it could be some other sort of code, but the simplest way to do it would be to pick one the languages and use its words to mark the meaning. Thus, for example, we could take 'he', 'him', 'il', 'le', 'lui', and say that all of them are variants of the idea of 'he'. In fact, we don't have to use the words of only one of the languages throughout: we could use whichever word is the shortest of those offered by the two languages; for example, of 'quickly' and 'vite', we could say that they both represent the idea of 'vite', since 'vite' is shorter to type than 'quickly'. The third slot in our specification is suggested by the existence of the different word-forms taken by the idea 'he': which form is used depends on whether the word is acting as subject of a sentence or is fulfilling some other function. In 'I like her', 'her' is acting as the object of the verb; in 'Je parle francais avec lui', French requires 'lui' rather than 'il' or 'le' because it is fulfilling some third type of function, which for the sake of argument we shall call instrumental. These latter grammatical variations are usually referred to as Cases. Finally, each word must have its Part-Of-Speech indicated — noun, verb, adjective etc.

So we already have quite a string of categories which must appear in any adequate specification for a sentence in English or French:

Part-of-speech, language, root, case, person, number, gender.

Let's try to specify a few words, using these labels.

(1) 'he': pronoun, English, he, subject, 3rd, singular, masculine.
(2) 'him': pronoun, English, he, object, 3rd, singular masculine.

(3) 'il': pronoun, French, he, subject, 3rd, singular, masculine.
(4) 'le': pronoun, French, he, object, 3rd, singular masculine.
(5) 'lui': pronoun, French, he, instrumental, 3rd, singular, masculine.

Using the grammar kit developed in the first section of this chapter, this translates quite easily into micro-PROLOG. However, it will look much better later on in display if the grammar kit is edited as outlined at the end of that section, so as to eliminate grammatical labels. Note that the grammar-kit allows you to include '/*' statements to remind yourself what your variables stand for. We shall be using this later on.

    vocab((pronoun he e he subj (3 s m)))
    vocab((pronoun him e he ojb (3 s m)))
    vocab((pronoun il f he subj (3 s m)))
    vocab((pronoun le f he obj (3 s m)))
    vocab((pronoun lui f he instr (3 s m)))

In fact, we have jumped right in at the deep end here: few other types of word are as complex as pronouns, with the exception of verbs. Starting thus, however, will mean that we won't have to go back and revise over-simplified material later.

As a contrast, let's try something a bit simpler: the words 'the', 'le', 'la', 'l'', and 'les'. Linguists refer to these as 'determiners' ('det' for short). They are never used with words that change with Person, only with nouns, which are all Third Person. So we can leave out the Person category in specifying determiners. Nor are they sensitive to Case: they stay the same whether they form part of the subject, object, or anything else. Our specification for these words, then, will consist of

    Part-of-speech, language, root, number, gender

thus:

    vocab((det the e the (x y)))
    vocab((det le f the (s m)))
    vocab((det la f the (s f)))
    vocab((det les f the (p x)))

In the first example, the 'x' indicates that 'the' can be any Number (i.e. either singular or plural), and the 'y' that it can be any Gender.

The fourth example says that 'les' can be any Gender.
Nouns are no different.

vocab((noun man e man (s m)))
vocab((noun men e man (p m)))
vocab((noun homme f man (s m)))
vocab((noun hommes f man (p m)))

This gives us the material with which to formulate the rules for Noun Phrases (np). One kind of np is the pronoun on its own. Another is the determiner and a noun together. Let's stick at those two for the moment:

rule((np X Y Z x)
   (pronoun X Y Z x)
   (/* (X lang) (Y root) (Z case) (x png)))

rule((np X (Y1 Y2) Z (3 | x1))   /* As above, but we have speci-
                                     fied that the
   (det X Y1 x1)   /* Person of this type of np will
                                     always be
   (noun X Y2 x1)   /* Third Person.
   (/* (Y1 det root) (Y2 noun root)))

Stage two: the Verb Phrase

Verbs are complicated beasts, but let's keep it simple to start with. We'll leave out all considerations of tense, and of auxiliary verbs (the 'am' in 'I am eating', for example). The simple present tense will do just fine, and we'll take a nice regular verb such as 'like'.

'Like' requires an object: we never say 'I like.'; rather, 'I like you.'. So our basic vp will consist of a verb and noun phrase. Straight away, however, we encounter an interesting problem, because when this object np consists of a pronoun, the English word order does not follow that of the French – 'I like you', but 'Je vous aime'. When the np consists of a determiner and a noun, however, English and French *are* similar.

First, though, the verb itself. As we mentioned earlier, it takes its cue from the subject; for example, if the subject is 'I', the verb will be 'like', but if the subject is 'he' or 'she' the verb will be 'likes'. So Person and Number will be important characteristics of the verb, and in French, the perfect tense is also sensitive to Gender, so we shall include that as well. Then we must allow for Language and Root, as with every type of word. And eventually, as hinted above, room will also have to be made for a number of other characteristics such as tense, but enough for now.

    vocab((verb likes e like (3 s x)))
    vocab((verb like e like (x s y)) (NOT EQ x 3))
    vocab((verb like e like (x p y)))
    vocab((verb aimes f like (2 s x)))
    vocab((verb aime f like (x s y)) (NOT EQ x 2))
    vocab((verb aimons f like (1 p x)))
    vocab((verb aimez f like (2 p x)))
    vocab((verb aiment f like (3 p x)))

So much for the verb. How do we put it together with an np to make a vp? First of all, we must deal with the special case of the French word-order when using pronoun objects. Then we shall cater for the more general cases. In fact, as a method of procedure, that is a common way to go about things in computing, since current processors read through the memory from the top down. Future computers with multiple processors working in parallel will make things interestingly different.

    rule((vp f Y Z (x y))
        (pronoun f x obj y)
        (verb f Y Z)
        (/∗ (Y verb root) (Z verb png) (x np root) (y png of np)))

    rule((vp X Y Z (x y))
        (/∗ (X lang))
        (verb X Y Z)
        (np X x obj y))

In fact, that won't work quite perfectly in its present form: try it and see if you can work out why.

Stage three: the whole sentence

Finally, we need to combine our np and our vp rules to make a sentence rule. The sentence rule must extract from np and vp all the necessary ingredients for generating a complete sentence in another language. That means noting all the Root meanings, the

Person and Number of the subject np and verb (but not the Gender, since what is feminine in French may not be feminine in English), similar details for the object np, and the language:

```
rule((sent X (Y1 Y2 Z) (x y))
     (/* (X lang)
         (Y1 subj np root)
         (Y2 verb root)
         (Z obj np details)
         (x y pn))
     (np X Y1 subj (x y z))
     (vp X Y2 (x y z) Z))
```

Two ways to translate

There are two ways you can approach the actual translation programs. First, you can ask for all possible sentences to be generated, together with their translations:

```
&. ((tr x)
    (FORALL ((sent X () e | z) (sent Y () f | z))
            ((PP) (PP | X) (PP | Y)) ))
```

The first use of *sent* generates an English sentence (e) with specification z; this specification is then used as the match against which the second use of *sent* generates its sentence in French (f). For each occasion this can be done, the text of the sentences is printed out.

Then you can also arrange things so as to input a specific sentence (all of whose words must be present in the memory), and get back the translation in the other language:

```
&. ((T x)
    (sent x () y | z)
    (flip y y1)
    (sent x1 () y1 | z)
    (PP) (PP | x1))
&. ((flip e f))
&. ((flip f e))
```

Again, the 'z' in both *sents* ensures that the sentence specifications match.

Example uses would be

&. tr x

and

&. T (THE MAN LIKES THE WOMAN)

and

&. T (JE AIME LE HOMME)

Obviously the last sentence is *wrong*! French has this annoying habit of chopping off vowels in certain circumstances. So my parting challenge to you is to improve these programs to the point where they can speak French 'as she is spoke'.

Appendix

Listed here are a number of modules discussed in various chapters of the book. We begin with the modules that contribute to turtle graphics.

trig-mod
This module provides SIN and COS values for those versions of micro-PROLOG that don't have them built in. It is a compromise between a short but slow program (for example, one which calculated the values each time, using some polynomial such as Tchebychev's), and a long but fast one. It is fairly long, listing all the SIN values from 0 to 90 inclusive, and using a simple adjustment to calculate all other values from that. You may well be able to do better.

```
&. ? ((CRMOD trig-mod (SIN COS absolute) (ed)))

trig-mod. ((SIN X Y)
            (adjust X Z x)
            (INT Z y)
            (sin y z)
            (TIMES x z Y))

trig-mod. ((COS X Y) (SUM 90 X Z) (SIN Z Y))
```

```
trig-mod. ((adjust X Y Z)
           (IF (LESS 360 Z)
               (   (SUM x 360 X)
                   (adjust x Y Z)
               )
               (   (LESS X 0)
                   (absolute X y)
                   (adjust y Y z)
                   (TIMES -1 z Z)
               )
           )
          )
trig-mod. ((adjust X Y 1)
           (LESS X 181)
           (IF (LESS X 91) ((EQ X Y))
                           ((SUM Y X 180)) ))
trig-mod. ((adjust X Y -1)
           (LESS 180 X)
           (SUM Z 180 X)
           (adjust Z Y x))

trig-mod. ((absolute X Y)
           (SIGN X Z)
           (TIMES X Z Y))
trig-mod. ((sin 0 0))
trig-mod. ((sin 1 0.01174524))
       etc. etc. etc.
trig-mod. ((sin 90 1))
trig-mod. CLMOD x
&.
```

turt-mod

'turt-mod' together with 'trig-mod' will give you turtle graphics.

```
&. ? ((CRMOD turt-mod (cls fd bk tn face drto jumpto repeat rem
                      callit make round rot pdata sum times
                      pen ink paper append "?ERROR?")
                     (SIN COS PEN INK PAPER pos dir coord
                      absolute coords up down ed)))

turt-mod. ((cls 8) (CLS 7) (NORMAL x))
turt-mod. ((cls X) (cls X X 0))
turt-mod. ((cls X Y Z)
           (ready screen X Y Z)
           (ready turtle))

turt-mod. ((ready screen X Y Z)
           (CLS X)
           (HYBRID x)
           (paper Y)
           (ink Z))
turt-mod. ((ready turtle)
           (pen down)
           (ch-pos (0 0))
           (face 0)
           (KILL coord)
           (turton))

turt-mod. ((fd X)
           (dir Y)
           (move X Y))
```

```
turt-mod. ((bk X)
            (tn 180)
            (fd X)
            (tn 180))

turt-mod. ((move X Y)
            (! destination X Y Z)
            (IF (PEN down)
                ((drto Z))
                ((jumpto Z)) ))

turt-mod. ((destination X Y Z)
            (SIN Y x)
            (COS Y y)
            (rot (X 0) (x y) z)
            (adjust z Z))

turt-mod. ((drto X)
            (pos Y)
            (turtoff)
            (line Y X)
            (! moveturt X))

turt-mod. ((jumpto X)
            (turtoff)
            (! moveturt X))

turt-mod. ((rot X Y (Z x))
            (rotx X Y Z)
            (roty X Y x))

turt-mod. ((rotx X (Y Z) x)
            (calculate TIMES X (Z Y) (y z))
            (SUM X1 z y)
            (round X1 x))

turt-mod. ((roty X Y Z)
            (calculate TIMES X Y (x y))
            (SUM x y z)
            (round z Z))

turt-mod. ((adjust X Y)
            (pos Z)
            (calculate SUM X Z Y))

turt-mod. ((line X (Y Z))
            (pdata x)
            (append X (Y Z x) y)
            (LNE|y))

turt-mod. ((pdata X)
            (PAPER Y)
            (INK Z)
            (TIMES 8 Y x)
            (SUM Z x X))

turt-mod. ((turton)
            (pos (X Y))
            (PNT X Y 184))

turt-mod. ((turtoff (X Y))
            (pdata Z)
            (PNT X Y Z))
```

```
turt-mod. ((turtoff)
           (pos X)
           (turtoff X))

turt-mod. ((moveturt X)
           (ch-pos X)
           (turton)
           (data))

turt-mod. ((tn X)
           (dir Y)
           (SUM X Y Z)
           (! face Z))

turt-mod. ((face X)
           (! ch-dir X)
           (data))

turt-mod. ((ch-dir X)
           (LESS X 0)
           (SUM X 360 Y)
           (ch-dir Y))
turt-mod. ((ch-dir X)
           (LESS 359 X)
           (SUM Y 360 X)
           (ch-dir Y))
turt-mod. ((ch-dir X)
           (make dir X))

turt-mod. ((ch-pos X)
           (IF (in-limits (X)
               ((make pos X))
               ((P "Sorry: off the screen")(PP)) ))

turt-mod. ((in-limits (X Y))
           (LESS -126 X)    /* These limits will be different
           (LESS X 126)     /* for different makes of computer.
           (LESS -66 Y)
           (LESS Y 86))

turt-mod. ((make X Y)
           (KILL X)
           (ADDCL ((X Y)) ))

turt-mod. ((sum X Y Z) (calculate SUM X Y Z))

turt-mod. ((times X Y Z) (calculate TIMES X Y Z))

turt-mod. ((calculate X (Y Z) (x y) (z X1))
           (X Y x z)
           (X Z y X1))

turt-mod. ((append () X X))
turt-mod. ((append (X|Y) Z (X|x)) (append Y Z x))

turt-mod. ((round X Y)
           (IF (LESS X 0)
               ((SUM -0.5 X Z))
               ((SUM 0.5 X Z)))
           (INT Z Y))
```

```
turt-mod. ((pen X) (make PEN X))
turt-mod. ((ink X) (make INK X))
turt-mod. ((paper X) (make PAPER X))

turt-mod. ((rem X) (pos Y) (ADDCL ((coord Y)) ))

turt-mod. ((repeat X Y) (absolute X Z) (! rep Z Y))

turt-mod. ((rep 0 X))
turt-mod. ((rep X Y)
                (? Y)
                (SUM 1 Z X)
                (rep Z Y))

turt-mod. ((callit X)
                (getco Y)
                (ADDCL ((coords X Y)) ))

turt-mod. ((getco (X|Y))
                (DELCL ((coord X)))
                (getco Y))
turt-mod. ((getco ()))

turt-mod. ((data)
                (pos X)
                (dir Y)
                (PP The turtle is at X)
                (PP heading Y degrees))

turt-mod. (("?ERROR?" X Y)
                (IF (EQ 13 X)
                    ()
                    ((PP Error X)(ABORT)) ))

turt-mod. CLMOD x
&.
```

hare-mod

This is the extension to the basic turtle which enables rotation, translation, and other transformations of the shapes drawn by the turtle. Many of its clauses are imported from 'turt-mod' or 'trig-mod'.

```
&. ? ((CRMOD hare-mod (rotate mod plot show)
            (SIN COS PAPER INK ed rot
                append pdata coords)))

hare-mod. ((rotate X Y Z)
                (SIN Y x)
                (COS Y y)
                (! mod X rot (x y) Z))

hare-mod. ((mod () X Y () ))
hare-mod. ((mod (X|Y) Z x (y|z))
                (? ((Z X x y)))
                (mod Y Z x z))
```

```
hare-mod. ((plot (X|Y))
          (pdata Z)
          (append (X|Y) (X) x)
          (plotx x Z))
hare-mod. ((plotx (X) Y))
hare-mod. ((plotx ((X Y) (Z x)|y) z)
          (LNE X Y Z x z)
          (plotx ((Z x)|y) z))
hare-mod. ((show (X|Y)) (? Y) (plot X))
hare-mod. CLMOD x
&.
```

An independent hare-mod

You may develop material that takes up so much room in your computer's memory that you do not have space for 'trig-mod', 'turt-mod' and 'hare-mod' as well. This, therefore, is a version of the hare that does not import any of its program clauses from the turtle.

Assuming you have been using the turtle and the other, dependent hare, you should type

```
&. KILL turt-mod
&. KILL hare-mod
&. SPACE x
```

before trying to load this hare; otherwise micro-PROLOG will signal Error 12, meaning that there is a name clash between material on board and material you are trying to load (if that happens, REMEMBER TO CLOSE whatever file you are loading). If you do not plan to rotate any of your shapes, you might as well KILL trig-mod as well: you will then have plenty of memory free.

When you come to save this module on tape or disc, remember to store it in a file that has a name different from that used for the other, dependent hare: you cannot have two files with the same name on the same disc or microdrive cartridge. I use SHARE for the dependent hare, and HARE for the independent one. It is quite all right, however, for both modules to have the same module-name, since you would never want to have them both loaded at the same time.

```
&. ? ((CRMOD hare-mod (rotate mod plot show cls make
                      sum times ink paper round)
              (SIN COS PAPER INK ed coords)))
```

Now type in the clauses listed for the other hare-mod, plus the ones that it uses from 'turt-mod', namely

rot   rotx   roty   calculate   round   pdata   append   ink   paper   make
cls   sum   times   ready

```
((cls 8) (CLS 7) (NORMAL x))
((cls X) (cls X X 0))
((cls X Y Z)
     (ready screen X Y Z))
```

Close off the module as normal, test it, and save it.

expert-mod
This module is discussed in the second part of the book. It provides a fairly general-purpose expert-system shell. If you feel that because of this some of the wording of the screen messages is too general, you can easily change it to suit your particular purpose.

```
&. ? ((CRMOD expert-mod (name diagnose what why why-not add
                        check-out learn-about clear "?ERROR?")
                       (ed true false implies category)))

expert-mod. ((name X) (diagnose X))

expert-mod. ((diagnose X)
             (clear X)
             (CL ((X|Y)|Z))
             (check-out X Y Z))
expert-mod. ((diagnose X)
             (learn-about X))

expert-mod. ((clear X)
             (CLS 7)
             (KILL (true false category))
             (add category X))

expert-mod. ((check-out X Y Z)
             (! check Z)
             (consultation X Y Z))

expert-mod. ((check X)
             (FORALL ((true Y)) ((test Y X)))
             (FORALL ((false Y)) ((NOT test Y X)) ))

expert-mod. ((test X Y)
             (OR ((member X Y)) ((implied-in X Y)) ))

expert-mod. ((consultation X Y () )
             (PP Your X appears to be)
             (P "   "|Y)
             (PP))
```

expert-mod. ((consultation X Y (Z|x))
               (true Z)
               (consultation X Y x))
expert-mod. ((consultation X Y (Z|x))
               (NOT true Z)
               (relevance X Z y)
               (IF (EQ y 1)
                   ((add true Z) (consultation X Y x))
                   ((IF (EQ y 0)
                       ((add false Z) (FAIL))
                       ((consultation X Y (Z|x)))))))

expert-mod. ((relevance X Y Z)
               (format X Y)
               (R Z)
               (PP))

expert-mod. ((format X Y)
               (PP)
               (PP Is the following true of your X?)
               (PP Enter 1 for true; 0 for false)
               (PP)
               (P "   "|Y))

expert-mod. ((add X Y) (ADDCL ((X Y))))

expert-mod. ((learn-about X)
               (CLS 7)
               (PP I'm afraid I can't help you)
               (ask-about X))

expert-mod. ((ask-about X)
               (get-answer Y)
               (add-spec X Y))

expert-mod. ((get-answer X)
               (PP)
               (PP Please tell me the answer IN BRACKETS)
               (R X))

expert-mod. ((add-spec X Y)
               (to-list Y Z)
               (get-spec Z x)
               (display X Z x)
               (ADDCL ((X|Z)|x)))

expert-mod. ((get-spec X Y)
               (CLS 7)
               (PP I know this about|X)
               (get-true Z)
               (PP)
               (PP|Z)
               (get-rest x)
               (append Z x Y))

expert-mod. ((get-true (X|Y))
               (DELCL ((true X)))
               (get-true Y))
expert-mod. ((get-true ()))

expert-mod. ((get-rest (X|Y))
               (spiel)

```
                (R Z)
                (IF (EQ Z 0)
                    ((FAIL))
                    ((EQ Z X) (get-rest Y)) ))
expert-mod. ((get-rest () ))

expert-mod. ((append () X X))
expert-mod. ((append (X|Y) Z (X|x)) (append Y Z x))

expert-mod. ((why X)
                (PP)
                (PP Because you said the following were true)
                (show true))
                (PP)
                (PP And the following were false)
                (show false))

expert-mod. ((show X)
                (FORALL ((X Y)) ((P " "|Y) (PP)) ))

expert-mod. ((why-not X)
                (category Y)
                (to-list X Z)
                (IF (CL ((Y|Z)|x))
                    ((compare Z x) (PP) (PP Z|x))
                    ((clear Y) (add-spec Y X)) ))

expert-mod. ((compare X Y)
                (pp 1 X)
                (FORALL ((true Z) (NOT test Z Y)) ((PP|Z)))
                (pp 2 X)
                (FORALL ((false Z) (test Z Y)) ((PP|Z)) ))

expert-mod. ((to-list X Y)
                (IF (OR ((VAR X)) ((LST X)))
                    ((EQ X Y))
                    ((EQ (X) Y)) ))

expert-mod. ((what X)
                (FORALL ((CL ((X|Y)|Z) )) ((PP|Y))))

expert-mod. (("?ERROR?" 2 X) (FAIL))
expert-mod. (("?ERROR?" X Y)
                (NOT EQ X 2)
                (PP Error: X)
                (ABORT))

expert-mod. ((spiel)
                (PP)
                (PP Please add characteristics)
                (PP one at a time IN BRACKETS)
                (PP or type 0 to finish)
                (PP))

expert-mod. ((implied-in X Y)
                (implies Z X)
                (member Z Y))

expert-mod. ((display X Y Z)
                (CLS 7)
                (PP X|Y)
                (PP|Z)
                (PP))
```

152 APPENDIX

```
expert-mod. ((member X (X|Z)))
expert-mod. ((member X (Y|Z)) (member X Z))
expert-mod. ((pp 1 X)
             (PP)
             (PP Because you said these things were true)
             (PP but they are NOT true of|X)
             (PP))
expert-mod. ((pp 2 X)
             (PP)
             (PP And you said these things were false)
             (PP but they are NOT false of|X)
             (PP))
expert-mod. CLMOD x
&.
```

dbase-mod

'dbase-mod' is the subject of the second half of the chapter on databases. It helps you set up a database, and retrieve information from it.

```
&. ? ((CRMOD dbase-mod (add delete edit which item member
                       length append "?ERROR?")
                   (ed fields category)))
dbase-mod. ((add X)
            (reset category X)
            (CLS 7)
            (get-fields X Y)
            (add-spec X Y))
dbase-mod. ((reset X|Y)
            (KILL X)
            (ADDCL ((X|Y)) ))
dbase-mod. ((get-fields X Y)
            (IF (CL ((fields X Y)))
                ()
                ((blurb 1)
                 (mk-fields Y)
                 (ADDCL ((fields X Y)) )) ))
dbase-mod. ((mk-fields (X|Y))
            (R Z)
            (IF (EQ Z 0)
                ((FAIL))
                ((EQ Z X) (blurb 2) (mk-fields Y)) ))
dbase-mod. ((mk-fields () ))
dbase-mod. ((blurb 1)
            (CLS 7)
            (PP Please type name of first field)
            (PP))
dbase-mod. ((blurb 2)
            (PP)
            (PP Next field, or 0 to finish)
            (PP))
```

```
dbase-mod. ((add-spec X Y)
            (get-spec Y (Z|x))
            (display X Z x)
            (ADDCL ((X|Z)|x)))
dbase-mod. ((get-spec () () ))
dbase-mod. ((get-spec (X|Y) (Z|x))
            (CLS 7)
            (PP Now type in X IN BRACKETS)
            (read X Z)
            (get-spec Y x))
dbase-mod. ((display X Y Z)
            (CLS 7)
            (PP X|Y)
            (PP|Z)
            (PP))
dbase-mod. ((read X Y)
            (PP)
            (P X:)
            (R Z)
            (PP)
            (to-list Z Y))    /* In case list-brackets omitted,
                              /* but only works for single words.
dbase-mod. ((to-list X Y)
            (IF (OR ((LST X)) ((VAR X)))
                ((EQ X Y))
                ((EQ (X) Y)) ))
dbase-mod. ((delete X)
            (to-list X Y)
            (category Z)
            (DELCL ((Z|Y)|x) ))
dbase-mod. ((which (X|Y))
            (PP)
            (FORALL ((? Y)) ((PP X)) ))
dbase-mod. ((item X Y Z)
            (NUM X)
            (SUM 1 x X)
            (append y (Z|z) Y)
            (length y x))
dbase-mod. ((item X Y Z)
            (VAR X)
            (append x (Z|y) Y)
            (length x z)
            (SUM 1 z X))
dbase-mod. ((member X (X|Y) ))
dbase-mod. ((member X (Y|Z)) (member X Z))
dbase-mod. ((length X Y) (len X 0 Y))
dbase-mod. ((len () X X)
dbase-mod. ((len (X|Y) Z x)
            (SUM 1 Z y)
            (len Y y x))
dbase-mod. ((append () X X))
dbase-mod. ((append (X|Y) Z (X|x)) (append Y Z x))
```

154 APPENDIX

```
dbase-mod. ((edit X)
            (category Y)
            (CL ((Y|X)|Z) 1 x)
            (RFILL (((Y|X)|Z)) y)
            (ADDCL y x)
            (DELCL Y x))
dbase-mod. (("?ERROR?" 2 (X|Y))
            (PP)
            (PP Please define X)
            (PP)
            (R Z)
            (ADDCL Z)
            (? ((X|Y)) ))
dbase-mod. (("?ERROR?" X Y)
            (NOT EQ X 2)
            (PP Error : X)
            (ABORT))
dbase-mod. CLMOD x
&.
```

rules-mod

'rules-mod' is the companion to 'dbase-mod' that helps you write your rules for database enquiry. See the chapter in part two for a discussion of what it does. Note that it imports a number of clauses from 'dbase-mod', rather than duplicating them; so it will not work without 'dbase-mod' loaded.

```
&. ? ((CRMOD rules-mod (rules-for)
       (ed rules category fields item "?ERROR?")))

rules-mod. ((rules-for X)
            (CL ((X|Y)|Z))
            (fields X x)
            (spiel x)
            (get-format x y)
            (mk-rules X x y))
rules-mod. ((spiel X)
            (blurb 1 X)
            (blurb 2 X))
rules-mod. ((get-format X (Y|Z))
            (PP)
            (R x)
            (IF (EQ x 0)
                ((FAIL))
                ((EQ x Y) (spiel2 X) (get-format X Z)) ))
rules-mod. ((get-format X () ))
```

```
rules-mod. ((mk-rules X Y ())
            (list rules))
rules-mod. ((mk-rules X Y ((Z x y)|z))
            (/*    (X category)
                   (Y list of fields)
                   (Z relation-name of first rule))
            (mk-rule X Y (Z x y))
            (update rules Z)
            (mk-rules X Y z))
rules-mod. ((mk-rule X Y (Z x y))
            (get-pos Y (x y) (z X1))
            (ADDCL ((Z Y1 Z1)
                    (CL ((X|x1)|y1))
                    (! item z (x1|y1) Y1)
                    (! item X1 (x1|y1) Z1)
                    (/* (Y1 x) (Z1 y) )) ))
rules-mod. ((update X|Y)
            (IF (CL ((X|Y)) )
                ()
                ((ADDCL ((X|Y)) )) ))
rules-mod. ((get-pos X (Y Z) (x y))
            (item x X Y)
            (item y X Z))
rules-mod. ((list X)
            (FORALL ((X Y)) ((PP) (LIST Y)) ))
rules-mod. ((spiel2 X)
            (blurb 1 X)
            (blurb 3 X))
rules-mod. ((blurb 1 X)
            (CLS 7)
            (PP OK: these are your fields)
            (PP)
            (PP X)
            (PP))
rules-mod. ((blurb 2 X)
            (PP Now give me the form of the)
            (PP rules you want, IN BRACKETS)
            (PP)
            (PP Each must have three words)
            (PP with the relation-name first)
            (PP)
            (PP EG (author-of title author))
            (PP))
rules-for. ((blurb 3 X)
            (PP)
            (PP Next rule, or 0 to finish))
rules-mod. CLMOD x
&.
```

gram-mod

This is the module discussed in the chapter on generating sentences and translating from one language to another. Most of what it does is to speed the process of sentence analysis by inserting two extra arguments at strategic proints.

The import list is particularly long because it has to try and foresee all the grammatical labels anyone using the module is likely to pick — obviosuly a bit of a gamble!

```
&. ? ((CRMOD gram-mod (rule vocab generate "?ERROR?")
         (ed sent np vp noun det adj adjp adv advp adverb verb vb
          prep aux nuc perf prog modal mod mv verbal vbl prn pro pronoun)))
gram-mod. ((rule X) (rulex X Y) (ADDCL Y))
gram-mod. ((rulex ((X|Y)|Z) ((X (X x) y|Y)|z))
             (body Z (x y) z))
gram-mod. ((body ((X|Y) (Z|x)) (y z) ((X y z|Y) (Z|x)))
             (SYS Z))
gram-mod. ((body ((X|Y)) (Z x) ((X Z x|Y)) ))
gram-mod. ((body ((X|Y)|Z) x ((X|Y)|y))
             (SYS X)
             (body Z x y))
gram-mod. ((body ((X|Y)|Z) (x y) ((X x z|Y)|X1))
             (body Z (z y) X1))
gram-mod. ((vocab ((X Y|Z)|x))
             (caps Y y)
             (ADDCL ((X (X y|z) z|Z)|x) ))
gram-mod. ((caps X Y)
             (STRINGOF Z X)
             (to-caps Z x)
             (STRINGOF x Y))
gram-mod. ((caps X X))
gram-mod. ((to-caps () () ))
gram-mod. ((to-caps (X|Y) (Z|x))
             (IF (between a "z" X)
                 ((capital X Z))
                 ((EQ X Z)))
             (to-caps Y x))
gram-mod. ((between X Y Z)
             (NOT LESS Z X)
             (NOT LESS Y Z))
gram-mod. ((capital X Y)
             (CHAROF X Z)
             (SUM x 32 Z)
             (CHAROF Y x))
gram-mod. ((generate X)
             (FORALL ((sent X ()|Y)) ((sp X)) ))
```

```
gram-mod. ((sp (sent (np X vp Y)))
           (spr X Y))
gram-mod. ((sp (sent (np X)))
           (append Y (vp Z) X)
           (spr Y Z))

gram-mod. ((spr X Y)
           (PP)
           (PP NP X)
           (PP VP Y))
gram-mod. ((append () X X))
gram-mod. ((append (X|Y) Z (X|x)) (append Y Z x))

gram-mod. (("?ERROR?" 2 (X|Y))
           (CLS 7)
           (PP)
           (PP Please define X)
           (PP using rule or vocab)
           (R Z)
           (R x)
           (? ((Z x)))
           (? ((X|Y)) ))
gram-mod. (("?ERROR?" X Y)
           (NOT EQ X 2)
           (PP Error: X)
           (ABORT))

gram-mod. CLMOD x
&.
```

Blocksworld

Blocksword is not a module like the other programs listed here. This is so that you can get at it easily and modify it.

```
                    /* START */
&. ((start x)
    (cls 7)
    (putback table tower)
    (/* You can add other structures besides table and tower))

&. ((cls 8) (NORMAL x) (CLS 7))
&. ((cls X) (HYBRID x) (CLS X))

        /* THESE ARE THE SETTING-UP COMMANDS AND THE INITIAL /*
        /* DATABASE DESCRIBING THE STATE OF THE WORLD */

&. ((putback table|X)
    (/* X is a list of structures)
    (KILL (at on holding))
    (ADDCL ((at (-120 -65) table))
    (clear table)
    (FORALL ((member Y X)) ((build (Y table) )) ))
```

APPENDIX

```
&. ((clear table)
    (KILL occupied)
    (FORALL ((slots|X) (member (Y Z) X))
        ((ADDCL ((occupied Y (Z -65) no)) )) )
    (/* (X=list of slots)(Y=slot name)(Z=x-coord) ))

&. ((switch X Y)
    (DELCL ((occupied X Z x)))
    (ADDCL ((occupied X Z Y)) ))

&. ((slots (A -120)(B -90)(C -60)(D -30)(E 0)(F 30)(G 60)(H 90) ))

&. ((build (X Y))
    (structure X Z)
    (reserve-space x)
    (bld Z Y x)
    (view x))

&. ((bld () X Y))
&. ((bld (X|Y) Z (x y))
    (/* (X=first object)(Z supports X)((x y)=coords))
    (ADDCL ((on Z X)))
    (ADDCL ((at (x y) X)))
    (size X z)
    (SUM z y X1)
    (bld Y X (x X1) ))

&. ((size m 20))
&. ((size c 20))
&. ((size g 20))
&. ((size n 20))
&. ((size e 25))
&. ((size triangle 20))
&. ((size tub 25))

&. ((shape m square))
&. ((shape c square))
&. ((shape g square))
&. ((shape n square))
&. ((shape e square))
&. ((shape triangle triangle))
&. ((shape table table))
&. ((shape tub tub))

&. ((structure tower (c m g) ))
&. ((structure spire (n triangle) ))
&. ((structure stand (e tub) ))

    /* NOW COME THE COMMANDS FOR CHANGING THE STATE OF THE WORLD /*

&. ((pickup X)                          /* PICKUP */
    (NOT holding Y)
    (NOT on X Z)
    (DELCL ((on x X)))
    (ADDCL ((holding X)))
    (hang X (0 80) ))
&. ((pickup X)
    (holding Y)
    (error still holding Y))
&. ((pickup X)
    (on X Y)
    (error Y still on X))
```

```
&. ((pickup X)
      (ADDCL ((holding X)) ))
&. ((letgo X)                              /* LETGO */
      (DELCL ((holding X)))
      (IF (on Y X)
          ()
          ((DELCL ((at Z X)) )) ))
&. ((letgo X)
      (NOT holding X)
      (error not holding X))


&. ((place (X table))                      /* PLACE */
      (IF (holding X)
          ((reserve-space Y)(reposition X table Y))
          ((error not holding X)) ))
&. ((place (X Y))
      (NOT EQ Y table)
      (holding X)
      (NOT on Y Z)
      (top-left Y x)
      (reposition X Y x))
&. ((place (X Y))
      (NOT EQ Y table)
      (on Y Z)
      (error Z still on Y))
&. ((place (X Y))
      (NOT holding X)
      (error not holding X))

                    /* ERROR MESSAGES */

&. ((error|X)
      (PP) (PP Sorry:|X) (PP) (ABORT))

                    /* TOP-LEFT COORD OF SQUARE */

&. ((top-left X (Y Z))
      (shape X square)
      (size X x)
      (at (Y y) X)
      (SUM x y Z))
&. ((top-left X Y)
      (error bad shape))

&. ((hang X (Y Z))                         /* POSITION AFTER 'PICKUP' */
      (size X x)
      (SUM y x Z)
      (free slot X)
      (ADDCL ((at (Y y) X)) ))

&. ((free slot X)
      (DELCL ((at Y X)))
      (IF (occupied Z Y yes)
          ((switch Z no)) () ))

&. ((reposition X Y Z)                     /* POSITION AFTER 'PLACE' */
      (ADDCL ((on Y X)))
      (DELCL ((at x X)))
      (ADDCL ((at Z X)) ))
```

160 APPENDIX

```
&. ((reserve-space X)                    /* MISCELLANEOUS UTILITIES */
    (occupied Y X no)
    (switch Y yes))

&. ((data X)
    (PP)
    (FORALL ((on Y Z)) ((P (Z on Y)" "))
    (PP)
    (IF (holding x)
        ((PP (holding x) )) () ))

&. ((ch-size (X Y))
    (DELCL ((size X Z)))
    (ADDCL ((size X Y)) ))

&. ((member X (X|Y) ))
&. ((member X (Y|Z)) (member X Z))

&. (("?ERROR?" 2 X)(FAIL))
&. (("?ERROR?" X Y)
    (NOT EQ X 2)
    (PP Error X)
    (ABORT))

                    /* THESE ARE THE DRAWING COMMANDS */
&. ((view X)
    (/* X is a throw-away argument)
    (cls 7)
    (FORALL ((at Y Z)) ((shape Z x)(draw x Z Y)) ))

&. ((draw table X (Y Z))
    (SUM Y 240 x)
    (SUM Z 1 y)
    (top Y Z x y)
    (legs Y Z x))

&. ((draw square X (Y Z))
    (size X x)
    (SUM x Y y)
    (SUM x Z z)
    (sq Y Z y z)
    (label X (Y Z) ))

&. ((draw triangle X (Y Z))
    (size X x)
    (SUM x Y y)
    (SUM x Z z)
    (TIMES 2 X1 x)
    (SUM X1 Y Y1)
    (LNE Y Z y Z)
    (LNE Y Z Y1 z)
    (LNE Y1 z y Z))

&. ((draw tub X (Y Z))
    (size X x)
    (SUM x Y y)
    (SUM x Z z)
    (LNE Y Z y Z)
    (LNE Y Z Y z)
    (LNE y Z y z))

&. ((top X Y Z x)
    (LNE X Y Z Y)
    (LNE X x Z x))
```

```
&. ((legs X Y Z)
      (SUM 23 X x)
      (SUM y 23 Z)
      (SUM z 10 Y)
      (LNE x Y x z)
      (LNE y Y y z))

&. ((sq X Y Z x)
      (LNE X Y X x)
      (LNE X Y Z Y)
      (LNE Z x X x)
      (LNE Z x Z Y))

&. ((label X (Y Z))
      (SUM 5 Y x)
      (SUM 5 Z y)
      (write X (x y)))

&. ((write c (X Y))
      (SUM X 7 Z)
      (SUM Y 10 x)
      (LNE X Y X x)
      (LNE X Y Z Y)
      (LNE X x Z x))
&. ((write g (X Y))
      (SUM X 7 Z)
      (SUM Y 10 x)
      (SUM Y 3 y)
      (SUM z 3 Z)
      (LNE X Y X x)
      (LNE X Y Z Y)
      (LNE Z Y Z y)
      (LNE Z y z y)
      (LNE Z x X x))
&. ((write m (X Y))
      (SUM X 8 Z)
      (SUM Y 10 x)
      (SUM X 4 y)
      (SUM Y 5 z)
      (LNE X Y X x)
      (LNE X x y z)
      (LNE y z Z x)
      (LNE Z x Z Y)
      (PNT X Y))
&. ((write e (X Y))
      (SUM 10 X Z)
      (SUM 10 Y x)
      (SUM 5 Y y)
      (LNE X Y Z Y)
      (LNE X Y X x)
      (LNE X x Z x)
      (LNE X y Z y))
&. ((write n (X Y))
      (SUM 10 X Z)
      (SUM 10 Y x)
      (LNE X Y X x)
      (LNE X x Z Y)
      (LNE Z Y Z x)
      (PNT X Y))
```

Index

ABORT, 42, 53, 70-71
absolute, 50
add, 121, 152
ADDCL, 39, 40, 68
addition, 31, 49
adjective phrase, 128-129, 131-132
adverb phrase, 128-129, 131-132
alphabet, 110-111
append, 62-64, 68
argument, 32-35
arithmetic, 49-52
ASCII code, 47
ask-about, 118
asking questions, 19-20

backtracking, 20-30, 57
bar graph, 105-106
bar sign '|', 56
blocksworld, 99-100, 157-161
BORDER, 48
brass (orchestral), 67
bread-slicer, 56
break, 18
brother, 69

callit, 107-108, 147
capital, 47, 130

cartesian geometry, 106-110
case (grammar), 137
category, 114, 115, 117, 121
CHAROF, 47
chicken, 95-98
circle, 103, 104
CL, 68-80, 117, 126
clam, 109-110
clause, 17
CLMOD, 83-88
CLOSE, 41, 87
CLS, 48
cls, 48, 102, 105-106
CON, 52
constant, 35
COS, 143-144
CRMOD, 83-85, 88
cross river, 98

databases, 113-126
dbase-mod, 152-154
DELCL, 39, 68
delete, 124, 153
diagnose, 114, 149
DICT, 41, 88
division, 49
drto, 106-107, 145

ed, 84, 86-87
ed-mod, 84
edit, 124-125, 154
empty list '()', 43, 55, 56, 61, 62
EQ, 30, 41, 42
error 2, 19, 69-73
error 6, 41, 87
error 11, 18, 88
error 12, 87, 148
error 13, 53, 101
error-trapping, 63, 68-80
euclidean geometry, 101-106
exclamation mark '!', 53, 80, 81
expert, 113-119
expert-mod, 149-152
export list, 84-88

face, 103, 146
factorial, 52
FAIL, 42, 59
failure, 20-30, 59
family, 69, 80
family tree, 69-80
farmer, 95
fd, 101, 144
female, 78–80
fields, 119-123
files,
    closing, 41, 87
    error 6, 41, 87
    loading, 41, 87-89
    naming, 40-41
    saving, 40-41, 84-85, 87
find, 74-79
FORALL, 33, 35, 45-46, 59
fox, 95-98
full boat, 45, 96

gender, 136, 137
generate, 132-133, 135-136
geometry, 101-110
get in, 95-98
get out, 95-98
give a value to, 21, 31
grain, 95-98
gram-mod, 156-157

grammar, 127-142
graphics, 48
    Blocksworld, 99-100
    Turtle graphics, 101

HARE, 148
hare, 108-110
hare-mod, 147-149
horizontal, 110-111
HYBRID, 48

IF, 42-44
import list, 84-88
ink, 105-106
input and output, 37-38, 66
instantiation, 21, 29, 34
insult, 93-94
INT, 50, 51, 52
interrupt, 18, 88, 93
intersection, 65-66
ISALL, 45, 96
item, 63-65, 67

jumpto, 106-107, 145

KILL, 39, 86, 88
known-female, 78-80
known-male, 78-80

learn-about, 118
learn-as-you-go, 73-80
length, 60-61
LESS, 47-50
letgo, 99-100, 159
LIST, 38, 41, 86, 88
lists,
    append, 62-64, 68
    bar sign '|', 56
    empty, 43, 55, 56, 61, 62
    format of, 17-18, 56-57, 67, 125-126
    heads and tails, 56, 59
    item, 63-65, 67
    length, 60-61
    member, 57-58
    nested, 67
    reverse, 61-62

updating
    (ADDCL, DELCL), 39, 40, 68
LNE, 48
LOAD, 41, 87-89
load (fox etc), 97
local variables, 30, 31
logic, 13, 20, 60
lower case, 130
LST, 52

male, 78-80
maths, 49-52
member, 57-58
mod, 109, 110, 147
modules,
    closing, 83-88
    creating, 83-85, 88
    editing, 87
    error 12, 87, 148
    export list, 84-88
    import list, 84-88
    killing, 86, 88
    naming, 84-85
    opening, 83-88
    saving, 84-89
move, 99
multiplication, 31, 49

name, 114, 119
newline command, 38
NORMAL, 48
noun phrase, 128-141
NOT, 42
np, 128-141
NUM, 52, 63
number (grammar), 137, 138

object (grammar), 139, 140
oneof, 93-94
OPMOD, 83-88
OR, 44, 151
orchestra, 67
order of rules, 81-82

P, 37-38
PP, 19-20, 37-38, 66

packaging, 19, 94
paper (turtle), 105-106
part-of-speech, 137
pattern, 105
pattern2, 109
pen (turtle), 105
pentagon, 102
person (grammar), 137
pickup, 99-100, 158
place, 99-100, 159
plot, 110, 148
PNT, 48
poly, 102-103
poultry, 57-60, 66, 68
power, 51
predicate, 20, 34-35

queries, 19-20
query-the-user, 73-80
question mark '?',
    solve, 19, 53
    failure, 21, 28, 39

R, 37, 38
rect, 103-104
recursion, 58, 81-82
relation-name, 34-35
rem, 107-108, 147
remarks '/*', 33, 43, 53
repeat, 101, 147
requests, 19-20
reverse, 61-62
rivergame, 95-99
RND (random numbers), 50, 51
root (grammar), 137, 138
rotate, 109, 147
round, 51
rounding, 50, 51
row across, 96
rule (grammar), 129-141
rule ordering, 81-82
rules (micro-PROLOG), 31-33, 67, 122-123, 125
rules-for, 122, 154
rules-mod, 154-155

SAVE, 40-41, 84-85
seafood, 57-60
sent (grammar), 131-141
sets, 65-66
SHARE, 148
show, 109-110, 148
sibling, 69
SIGN, 50, 51
SIN, 143-144
sloping, 110
SPACE, 53, 88
spiral, 105
sq, 101
square, 107, 108, 109
stack, 81
star, 104
STRINGOF, 46-47
strings (characters), 46
strings (orchestral), 67
subtraction, 49
success, 20-30
SUM, 31, 49
SYS, 52, 129-130

T (translating), 141-142
tail recursion, 58, 81-82
take (fox etc), 99
teaching the computer, 17
throw-away argument, 94, 95, 107
TIMES, 31, 49
tn (turning turtle), 101, 146
to-caps, 156
to-list, 52, 117, 153
topics, 122, 123
tr (translating lang), 141-142
transformation,
    (geometry), 107-110

translation,
    geometry, 107, 109-110
    language, 136-142
trig-mod, 143-144, 148
turt-mod, 144-147
turtle, 110-111
two-word sentences, 19
type testing, 52

union, 65-66
unload (fox etc), 97
update, 43
upper case, 130

VAR, 52, 64, 65, 151
variables, 30-35
verb phrase, 128-141
vertical, 110-111
vocab (grammar), 130-141
vp, 128-141

week, 63
weekdays, 63, 64, 68
weekend, 63, 64, 65, 68
which, 59-60, 123-124, 153
why, 113, 117
why-not, 113, 117-118

|, 56
!, 53, 80, 81
(), 43, 55, 56, 61, 62
/*, 33, 43, 53
? (failure), 21, 28, 29
? (solve), 19, 53
&, 17, 84
"?ERROR?", 42, 53-54, 71, 73, 79, 80